One-Room Schools in the Past

Helen Winters Wilson

A publication of

Eber & Wein Publishing

Pennsylvania

One-Room Schools in the Past

Copyright © 2019 by Helen Winters Wilson

Library of Congress
Cataloging in Publication Data

ISBN 978-1-60880-652-2

Proudly manufactured in the United States of America by

Eber & Wein Publishing

Pennsylvania

In Memory of Grandma and Mother
Mary Little Johnson and Margaret Johnson Winters

Grandma Mary was a school teacher and she resigned to marry my Grandpa George E. Johnson in 1907. Grandma was left-handed and her six children's education was very important in her life. They owned Johnson Dairy Farm located very close to Dallas Pike in West Virginia. It was a family business bottling their milk from their large herd of Jersey cows and delivering milk, cream, and butter each week to the city of Wheeling; it was an around-the-clock business. Grandma churned twice a week and getting the butter ready for delivery each week kept her daughters very busy.

My mother Margaret Elizabeth was the oldest girl. Her job was to care for her younger sister Florence and help with cooking while Merle and Clarence (or Buddy) helped milk the cows and tended to all work around the farm. When Florence was older she worked in the spring house bottling the milk.

Grandma's plans were to educate all her children. The boys would run the farm and her girls would become teachers. When my mother met my father Melvin, her plans for college changed; she married Melvin and moved to West Alexander, PA to another large farm. Mother never regretted her decision to be a farmer's wife and live in the country. She loved poetry and would walk through our home reciting many beautiful poems. I developed my love for poetry while listening to my mother.

Contents

Introduction...vii

Chapter 1..1
Stories about the One-Room Schools

Chapter 2..3
Knob School, West Finley Twp, Washington Co., PA

Chapter 3..6
Knob School, West Finley Twp, Washington Co., PA

Chapter 4..8
Knob School, West Finley Twp, Washington Co., PA

Chapter 5..11
Knob School, West Finley Twp, Washington Co., PA

Chapter 6..13
Knob School, West Finley Twp, Washington Co., PA

Chapter 7..15
Kimmins School, West Finley Twp, Washington Co., PA

Chapter 8..18
Kimmins School, West Finley Twp, Washington Co., PA

Chapter 9..20
Kimmins School, West Finley Twp, Washington Co., PA

Chapter 10..22
Kimmins School, West Finley Twp, Washington Co., PA

Chapter 11..24
History of the One-Room School

Chapter 12..26
Kimmins School, West Finley Twp, Washington Co., PA

Chapter 13..29
No. 2 School, Marshall Co., Dallas, WV

Chapter 14..33
No. 2 School, Marshall Co., Dallas, WV

Chapter 15..38
No. 2 School, Marshall Co., Dallas, WV

Chapter 16...41
    No. 2 School, Marshall Co., Dallas, WV

Chapter 17...43
    Oak Hill School, Marshall Co., Sand Hill, WV

Chapter 18...46
    Cooneytown School, West Finley Twp, Washington Co., PA

Chapter 19...49
    Gunn School, West Finley Twp, Washington Co., PA

Chapter 20...52
    Stoney Point School, East Finley Twp, Washington Co., PA

Chapter 21...55
    Dickerson School, South Franklin Twp, Washington Co., PA

Chapter 22...60
    Lindley School, South Franklin Twp, Washington Co., PA

Chapter 23...65
    Acton Corner, York Co., Acton, ME

Chapter 24...68
    Mace Hollow School, Madison Twp, Armstrong Co., PA

Chapter 25...72
    Glendale School, Ohio Co., Dallas Pike, WV

Chapter 26...77
    The Depression Lesson

Chapter 27...81
    Kimmins School, West Finley Twp, Washington Co., PA

Chapter 28...85
    Davidson School, West Finley Twp, Claysville, PA

Chapter 29...88
    Knob School, West Finley Twp, West Alexander, PA

Chapter 30...92
    Sand Hill, Marshall Co., Sand Hill, WV

Chapter 31...97
    William Holmes McGuffey

Introduction

The history of the one-room schools in the United States began with passage of the school law on May 8, 1854. The leading feature of the law was to establish the office of a superintendent to provide the knowledge and control of the school system.

Duties of the early superintendent were many. They found many school houses that were in very bad condition. Important plans were in progress on proper ways to construct the early one-room schools; another was locating a carpenter to do the work.

Another interesting issue were teachers with very little education. If a person wanted to teach they would take the books that were available in the school system, study the books, and they were ready to teach. The superintendent would go to the school early in spring to interview the person who applied for the teaching position.

Several teachers were rejected who weren't qualified to teach reading, writing, and arithmetic, which were the requirements. Another was the marriage issue. If a woman was married they were not qualified to teach.

In the early days it was very difficult to get around to all of the schools. Many of the superintendents traveled by horse back through snow-covered roads. There were no means of communication except for by mail, and that took several days.

In 1890 the Teachers Institute was established. The superintendents thought the most important work was the examination of the teachers, and they were of the opinion that the only way to raise the standards of education was by a rigid system of examination. Schools were divided into districts and a teachers institute was held in each district. Well-known speakers were brought into the district. Parents Day was established in 1896 and by 1906 many parents and friends began visiting their school on that day.

Chapter 1
Stories about the One-Room Schools

While driving along a country road, I have always been interested in one-room schools I would see along the way. Around a bend in the road, sitting upon a hill and looking in the distance there was a hay stack. It seemed amazing that long ago many of my family members who have gone to their heavenly home attended these schools. In those days the requirements for an education were reading, writing, and arithmetic.

I would like to tell some of their stories. My grandmother Mary Little Johnson was born November 22, 1886 in West Finley Township, PA, close to the little town of Beham. Her parents were James and Elizabeth Little who were parents of ten children; Mary was the youngest. James was a farmer and the family raised most of their food on their 175-acre farm. Sister Laverne, her only sister, lost her life while standing in front of an open-grate stove. She had just turned around after putting a shovel of coal on the grate when her long skirt caught on fire. She was just eighteen years old.

Mary and her brothers attended the Cooneytown school four miles from home. They were driven to school in a buggy by brother Lynn. During the winter months a sled hitched to a team of horses and driven by their father took them to school.

The school was located on Dague Farm back off the main road just below the sheep shed where sheep grazed each summer. Mary's main interest in those days was to become a teacher. One of her friends was Nellie Wallace who went on to teach eighth grade at the West Alexander school. Some of her classmates were Earl Dague, Olive Gunn, George Jones, and Bessie Ferrell. Their teacher was Fern A. Travis.

Upon graduation, Mary attended the Claysville Teachers Institute in Claysville, PA, where she earned her diploma to teach. She was hired to teach at the Knob school near Beham where she taught a class of twenty-four students from 1904–1907. In fall 1907 she resigned from teaching and married George Elwood Johnson.

Chapter 2
Knob One-Room School, West Finley Township, Washington Co., PA

I was lucky to know my grandmother Mary Little Johnson who shared with me many stories about teaching at the Knob one-room school, which was located at that time around two miles from the little town of Beham. The Little family's country home was just a short distance from town. Many times Grandma walked to Clovis store.

She taught there after she graduated from Claysville Teacher Institute in Claysville, PA. Her brother Lynn took her to school in the family buggy—their only way of transportation besides riding a horse. She told me she did most of her studies at home when there was snow on the ground. Teaching in the family was very important and Grandma's mother Elizabeth wanted all of her children to do well in life.

Mary's first instructions from Mr. William Dague, the school president, was to teach the first grade children their ABCs. At that time, the ABCs were written above the blackboard, which was behind the teacher's desk. The first grade students that year were Deane Porter, Milt Clovis, and Frank Hess. Each student was given a slate and chalk for writing and their spelling was done on the blackboard.

The older children were all reading and several of them could read really well. The teacher before was Fern Travis who quit teaching when she got married in 1905. She had previously taught at the Cooneytown School two miles from Beham. In those days when a woman chose to get married, she had to give up teaching.

One of the older children was in charge of ringing the bell for recess and dusting the erasers each afternoon. One little girl liked to eat chalk and I kept her chalk on my desk. She was a cute little girl who cried for her mommy. I sent word home with her brother Floy, and the family chose to keep her home for another year. The McConnell family had a little baby at home, and Mrs. McConnell sent word with Daisy, thanking me for caring for little Doris.

The winter of 1906 was very cold and the creeks were frozen over. Nellie Clovis, who lived on what is known today as Ladleys Run Road, had been skating on a frozen creek and asked me if the children could come down and skate. I decided to take the children down one day during lunch hour. We watched Charlie Ferrell and Orville McConnell try out their new skates. Nellie had been skating for some time and we enjoyed her skating skills.

For Valentine's Day on February 14th the children made their own valentines. We decorated a large box with crepe paper and children made a valentine for each other and a very special valentine for their parents and teacher. I saved some of my valentines to show to my children. The valentines were handed out by Deane Porter and Frank Hess. Mrs. Porter brought a gallon of apple juice and ginger cookies and the children had little folding cups they carried in their pocket for their juice.

We exchanged names for Christmas with small gifts not to cost more than fifty cents. Most of the gifts were socks, gloves, and toys for the smaller children. Santa came and handed out the gifts to each one of the children as they told Santa what they wanted for Christmas. Daisy McConnell told Santa she wanted a baby doll for her sister. When Santa asked her what *she* wanted she told Santa that she would play with her sister's doll. In those days children shared their toys and never asked for much.

Two students Lillian and Gladys Hunter loved to sing. I asked them to prepare a closing song for our Christmas program and they chose "Up on the Housetop."

Up on the housetop reindeer pause,
Out jumped good old Santa Claus,
Down through the chimney with lots of toys,
All for the little ones Christmas joys,
Ho, ho, ho! Who wouldn't go!
Ho, ho, ho, Who wouldn't go!
Up on the house top, click, click, click,
Down through the chimney with good Saint Nick.
First comes the stocking of little Nell,
Oh, dear Santa fill it well,
Give her a dolly that laughs and cries,
One that will open and shut her eyes.
Up on the housetop click, click, click,
Down through the chimney with good Saint Nick.

The children all went home happy with a candy cane.

Chapter 3
Knob One-Room School, West Finley Township, Washington Co., PA

What is experience? It is a dear teacher and we can avoid paying the price of experience by learning what our teachers have set down for us in our books.

My grandmother Mary Selema Little Johnson was very good at poetry. This is one of her favorite poems. This is the first verse of "Come Little Leaves" by George Cooper: "Come, little leaves, said the wind one day. Come o'er the meadow with me and play. Put on your dresses of red and gold, for the summer is over and the days grow cold." "The Village Blacksmith" was another. Grandma taught the fifth grade these two poems.

The years she taught at the Knob school she taught several poems to children. Poetry was easy to teach as children responded to the rhyme or sounds and motions that rhyme. Children learn from each other she often told me. Thursday was poetry day and the children would stand beside their desk and recite their weekly poem.

Grandma told me she enjoyed teaching the younger children their numbers. *We want to learn our numbers so we can count money,* she often told the children. She brought some small change to class—buffalo nickels and several Lincoln pennies (inscribed on the front was "In God We Trust.") It was a lot of fun and the children really enjoyed the class.

The older children learned to add, subtract, multiply and divide. All instructions were done on the blackboard. With their slate and chalk in their hands, the children went up to the blackboard and copied their numbers; this class was for the fifth and sixth grade students.

Four students—Dora Clovis, Charles Ferrell, Orville McConnell, and Amanda Chase—were in seventh grade. In eighth grade I only had two—Dessie Donston and Harry Beatty.

April 23, 1907 was the last day of school and several parents came including Mrs. Ferrell and Mrs. Hunter who brought a picnic lunch. Mrs. Ferrell made two of her favorite apple pies and chicken sandwiches and Mrs. Hunter brought a large lemon cake. All closing activities were held inside, as it rained that morning.

Chapter 4
Knob One-Room School, West Finley Township, Washington Co., PA

My grandma always had a lot of interesting information to tell me about the times she taught at the Knob school. The school was near the little town of Beham not far from the West Virginia state line. A little information about the town: there was a Clovis grocery store, a doctor's office, Christian church, and a post office.

Mary had six brothers and one sister, Laverne, who lost her life when her dress caught fire while standing in front of an open grate stove; she was just eighteen. As a child, Mary loved to read and there were always good books and the daily newspaper in her home when she was a child.

Mary attended the Cooneytown one-room school, which was back through the woods just above the Dague sheep shed. There she graduated from eighth grade and attended Claysville Teachers Institute about fifteen miles from her home.

She graduated in spring of 1905 and was hired to teach at the Knob one-room school. William Dague, the school president, hired her and told her there would be around twenty-four students scheduled to attend school in fall term. She told Mr. Dague she had all the requirements and was ready to teach.

Here is Mary's story. On the first day of school, my dad James took me to the school house in a buggy. Mr. Dague was already at school and had the school supplies—chalk, erasers, two brooms, paper supplies, and twenty-five McGuffey spelling and reading books. I had three poem books I bought while shopping in Wheeling, and my plan was to teach poetry.

Little Leslie McConnell was one happy child. I gave certificates and stars to the children who received an A-plus in reading. Leslie told me she wanted to show her certificate to her mother. I felt bad her mother was not there to see that special moment. I had four of the McConnell children in school; they had an older brother and younger sister at home.

Austa Strope was very good at spelling; she always had her spelling words memorized. I let her help with the spelling class of the younger children. She was a student whom I could count on and she always had her hand up asking questions. In her family she was an only child; she would have made a wonderful teacher.

Harry Hunter was always whistling at lunch hour. He would entertain the children while they ate their lunch. He had musical talent and I got to talking to him about his whistle. He told me he was learning to play a banjo, and you guessed it, every Friday we were entertained by Harry and Helen Ferrell who sang with him. "Turkey in the Straw" and "Oh, Them Golden Slippers" were among their favorite songs. I heard later Harry played for many square dances in the community.

The Hess children, Lydia and Frank, lived real close to school and were my little helpers. Frank always carried in water from the dug well in a bucket with a long handle dipper; if children didn't have a folding cup they drank out of the dipper.

The school year ended April 24, 1906 and William Dague and J. L. Scherich were at school to hand three students—Austa Strope, Floy McConnell, and Harry Hunter—their eighth-grade diplomas. It rained that morning and all activities had to be held inside. The were five children who had perfect attendance; they were Nellie Clovis, Russell Wilson, Dessie Dunston, Deane Porter, and Harry Hunter.

On closing day, I left the children with this thought, "True worth is in being, not seemingly, in doing some good each day that goes by. There's nothing so kindly as kindness and nothing so royal as truth, and to always follow the path that is narrow and straight—that is the path you all should follow."

Chapter 5
Knob One-Room School, West Finley Township, Washington Co., PA

Many activities occurred during the time I taught at the Knob school, Mary often told me. I always started each morning with a prayer. This was one quote I taught each Monday morning: "Do the duty that is best. Leave unto the Lord the rest. Whenever a task is set for you, don't idly sit and view it, begin at once and do it."

Around the first of December 1906 the children began to talk about Christmas, which was in a couple of weeks. I wanted to have something special for the children and I talked to my dad James about cutting one of the blue spruce trees on our farm.

James thought that was a wonderful idea and my brother Lynn brought a cut tree in the sled with a tree stand that he made. Mother Elizabeth had some paper bells and she made chains for the tree out of the daily newspaper.

I asked each child to bring a little gift to put under the tree. It was usually a pair of gloves or socks. Dora Clovis's mother brought her peanut taffy and came to the party in her buggy with her three-year-old daughter Nellie seated beside her.

We sang Christmas carols as Dora handed each student one of the presents under the tree. Austa Strope and Gladys and Lillian Hunter sang the hymn "Silent Night." Outside we heard the jingling of bells and Santa Claus popped in the door with a large red sack flung over his back. The children all lined up to talk to him.

Lynn was waiting to take me home in the buggy. The bells were ringing on Topseys back as Dad always put the bells on Topsey at Christmastime. It was Christmas again and becoming a school teacher was always on my mind that Christmas.

At the Claysville Teacher Institute I had the chance to go to Wheeling, WV, to Kirk's Photo Center and have my picture taken. At the studio I asked Mr. Kirk to print my photo in a little frame that I gave to the students on April 23, 1907.

Chapter 6
Knob One-Room School, West Finley Township, Washington Co., PA

Many people ask me how the Knob one-room school got its name. My dad Melvin Winters told me that the early settlers gave the school its name because it was built around a bend in the road, or a knob, and referred to as a rounded hill or bend.

I instructed the children to have good habits, especially reading, and I would recite many interesting poems to them. I would say, "Live to learn and you will learn to live. Advance in learning as you advance in life."

Some of my quotations were "Books are the legacies that the genies leave to mankind to be delivered down from generation to generation as presents to those who are yet unborn," and the real object of education is to give children resources that they will endure as long as they live—habits that time will ameliorate, not destroy.

Milt Clovis, who was in eighth grade, was assigned to dust the erasers each afternoon just before I rang the last bell at three-thirty. Charley Ferrell was to help Milt put the erasers back on the blackboard and then they would go outside to play ball.

Dora and Nellie Clovis were Milt's sisters. They lived over a mile from school. Milt drove a buggy to school each day and tied the horse he called Brownie to the hitching post in back of school. In winter months he had Brownie hitched to a sled. Dora told how they wrapped up in quilts during the winter months to keep warm.

Amanda Chase, whose uncle was Wilson C. Chase, was always telling stories about the Civil War. She said, "Uncle Wilson spent two years fighting in the Civil War and was discharged in Wheeling, WV. He could not wait to get back to the Chase farm in Beham and marry his sweetheart Ella Gunn, who was from the little town of Burnesville." She said, "Uncle Wilson walked to Burnesville to get Ella and they were married the next day May 16, 1885 at the Methodist Church in Dallas, WV."

Frank Hess brought his marbles to school in his pocket and the boys would go out at recess and entertain themselves with a game of marbles that Frank made up.

Frank was full of adventure and many times I would catch him looking out the window. He told me he helped his dad milk two cows each evening. Each day Frank's dad Bill brought him and his kid sister Lydia to school in a buggy.

The children were always telling me stories about their home life. Deane Porter, who lived near Beham, was excited about Christmas and Santa Claus. She was afraid Santa would not stop at the house Christmas Eve. I had a little story to tell about that adventure; I told her to put a cookie out for Santa!

On April 25, 1908 another school year ended and I handed out the reports to children. Mr. William Dague was on hand to present the two eighth graders Milt Clovis and Orville McConnell their diplomas.

As I was planning on getting married in August to George E. Johnson I would not be returning to teach in the fall. This is what I told the children: Dear Pupils, "As your knowledge and experience broadens with your mental horizon, you will take upon yourself the duties and responsibilities of your intensified life. It is my hope that in moments of retrospection you will call to mind the lessons I have taught you and I will never forget as days go by all my pupils dear. My thoughts will wander back to you throughout the coming years. Your teacher, Mary Selema Little

Chapter 7
Kimmins One-Room School, West Finley Township, Washington Co., PA

The school board president was William Dague, treasurer Danial Sprawls, and secretary H. M. Lacoch assisted by Robert Clovis. The teacher was Adaline Golden.

The Kimmins one-room school was located on Tom Kimmins property in what is known today as the Old Brick Road. Mr. Kimmins was very interested in education for the children who lived in the area. The school was built around the turn of the century.

Building the school at that time took almost two years to construct. The lumber was from local trees that were cut down and hauled by horse and wagon to a saw mill that was located close to West Alexander and sawed into lumber. Approximately forty men worked long hours building the school. The plans for the structure of most of the one-room schools were always the same and included a chimney for the stove that sat in the middle of each school and belfry (or tower) for the bell to hang in. The bell was rung every morning—a reminder for the local children to come to school. The morning bell was usually rang by the teacher or local parent who was assigned that duty.

In the fall of 1908 the teacher who was to teach that year was Adaline Golden. The Harry Winters family lived just up the road from the school and Adaline boarded with them during the school year. She received very little wages as the money came from the parents and local taxes.

The Winters' two daughters Nellie Mae, who was nine, and Rena, who was in second grade, loved to walk to school each morning with their teacher. Rena was very good at spelling and she enjoyed reading interesting stories about country life on the farm. This was a part of one of Rena's poems: "In my quiet country home was my father busy all day plowing corn and raking hay. When autumn came, what joy to see the gathering for husking bee; I felt my life had its greatest charm, when I was living on the farm."

Nellie and Rena enjoyed walking with the Geho children Lucy, Bessie, and Thelma. Rena and Mary A. Erskine were good friends; both were in the second grade reading class. Mary's mother brought her to school in a buggy, as she lived over a mile, quite a distance beyond the middle creek road. After graduating from high school Mary became a grade school teacher and the Erskine road and covered bridge bares her name; the road is located in West Finley Township, Washington Co., PA.

Blanch Kiger and her brother Eddie came to school each day in a buggy driven by their dad Furman. As the family lived up a muddy lane, in winter months Furman was concerned about Blanch walking to school and he always had his horse and buggy ready each day to take them to school. Blanch and Eddie loved to sing and always had a special song they performed at many of the school functions.

Ona Chase lived with the Winters family. She was Margaret Winters sister and came to live with her sister and family when she was just a small child. Her mother Ella died of breast cancer. The Winters family shared their home with Ona's dad Wilson, a Civil War vet, and her two brothers Lester and Ralph.

At a Halloween party Ralph McCoy, who had a popcorn patch on the family farm, brought popcorn balls for the party. His mother Jane had bought candy corn at Gibson grocery store in town and she sent the candy and popcorn to the school party with Ralph, as she wanted the children to have a special treat to take home.

One day Lucy Geho had a toothache and was crying. As Adeline was also the school nurse, she always had aspirin tablets handy for any pain problems with the children. As it was raining that day her father came in the buggy and took the girls home. Lucy grew up and married Wishard Supler and moved to West Virginia. Thelma married Erville Ritchey and she became a mother to six children.

Chapter 8
Kimmins One-Room School, District No. 3
West Finley Township, Washington Co., PA

At Kimmins one-room school in fall of 1909 the school had new teachers William Hutchinson and Nellie B. Hunter. William lived on McGuffey Road, which was close to school, and taught during the first half of the school year; Nellie taught the last half of the school year, which ended the last day of April.

Up front, over the blackboard hung the American flag in all the one-room schools. First thing every morning the students stood beside their desk and recited the Pledge of Allegiance. They were taught respect for the American flag.

"I pledge allegiance to the flag of the United States of America and to the republic for which it stands, one nation, under God, indivisible with liberty and justice for all. Amen"

There were six Hewitt children—Grace, Olive, Roy, Charley, Ray, and Dan. Roy and Dan were twins and in fourth grade. Their mother brought their lunch to them each day. They lived up McGuffey Road and she came to school in the family buggy.

The past year a family moved up McGuffey Road from Parkersburgh, WV, by the name of Hopkins. They had four children. Fred and Charly were the new students that year. Fred was twelve and was in sixth grade and Charley was in eighth grade.

There were three students in eighth grade—Charley Hopkins, Grace Hewitt, and Ralph McCoy. Grace was very good at reading. Mr.

Hutchinson had her read a story out of the eighth grade McGuffey Reader and report on it. She received a certificate for her reading skills on graduation day. The teacher Nellie Hunter handed out the graduation certificates to Charley Hopkins, Grace Hewitt, and Ralph McCoy. Olive Hewitt was in seventh grade and had all A's on her report card and could recite all twelve of her multiplication tables. Mrs. Hewitt came to the April graduation.

Chapter 9
Kimmins One-Room School, District No. 3
West Finley Township, Washington Co., PA

The school board members that year were David Wood, H. M. Lacock, G. A. Atkinson, and Jesse Sprowls. School let out the last day of April after being in session for eight months.

In fall of 1913 the teacher was Eleanor Ewing, a recent graduate of Claysville Teachers Institute. This was her first teaching job at the Kimmins school.

That year my dad Harry Melvin Winters was in fourth grade and had just turned nine that fall and his sister Rena was eleven. The family had recently moved to their new home on Chambers Ridge Road, which was quite a distance from the school.

Rena loved to read especially out of the McGuffey reader and news came that fall that the students from the Knob would be coming to have a spelling bee. This was for the children in fourth and fifth grade. The school board president Mr. William Dague brought the fourth and fifth grade students from the Knob school in his sleigh.

Rena and Gladys Hunter from the Knob school won the spelling bee. Other students were Deane Porter and Nellie Clovis from the Knob School and Melvin Winters, Emmett Chambers, and Eliza Kennedy from the Kimmins school.

At the spelling bee, Nellie Clovis brought four dozen raisin cookies and shared them with all the children. Nellie said her mother baked the raisin cookies just yesterday.

On March 12, 1914 Melvin and Rena's little baby brother Harold Lee was born. It was a lot of excitement for Rena, as she wanted to stay home and help take care of her baby brother. The family lost Harold September 7, 1922. Harold took sick at school and was taken home by his school teacher in her buggy. Diphtheria caused the death of Harold Lee Winters when he was eight years old; he died in his mother's arms.

Chapter 10
Kimmins One-Room School, District No. 3
West Finley Township, Washington Co., PA

At the Kimmins one-room school in the fall of 1917 the teacher that year was Eleanor Ewing; this was her fourth year of teaching. She lived close by the school and came to school in her buggy with her horse she called Bell and tied her to the hitching post.

Eleanor started each day reading from the Bible, and the Lord's Prayer was recited by all the children as they bowed their heads. My dad Melvin remembered her as a teacher who taught him his arithmetic. She was very good with figures.

Melvin was thirteen and was in eighth grade that year. His school buddies were Emmett Chambers and Raymond Main. They used to share their lunch together in the fall under one of the poplar trees. Emmett liked to trade his sausage sandwich for ham.

When the weather was nice in the fall, Raymond would bring his ball and we boys had fun passing the ball to each other. John Amos, Roy Holmes, George Gray, Charley Main, and Emmett—we all had so much fun until Miss Ewing called us to come in.

At Christmastime Santa came for a visit in the afternoon and brought some candy and popcorn balls for us all. Before we went home we all sang "Jingle Bells" and "Santa Clause Is Coming to Town." We all went home very happy!

At Easter Miss Ewing went to Clover Farm Store in West Alexander in her buggy and bought us a chocolate Easter egg. Before we left for home she gave us our egg. Melvin walked with Emmett part of the way and they ate their Easter egg on the way.

Graduation day was on April 21, 1918. Melvin recalls school board president David Wood was at school to hand out certificates to all students. They were Emmett Chambers, Marinda Gray, Lucy Geho, Nellie Wood, Raymond Main, and George Gray. Lucy Geho and Marinda Gray received certificates for perfect attendance.

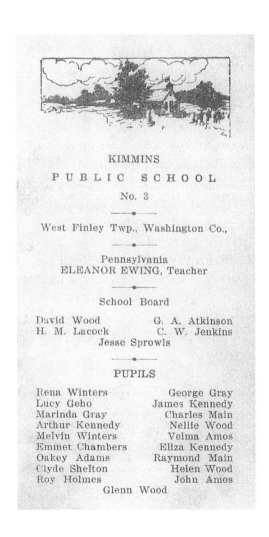

KIMMINS

P U B L I C S C H O O L

No. 3

West Finley Twp., Washington Co.,

Pennsylvania
ELEANOR EWING, Teacher

School Board

David Wood	G. A. Atkinson
H. M. Lacock	C. W. Jenkins
Jesse Sprowls	

PUPILS

Rena Winters	George Gray
Lucy Geho	James Kennedy
Marinda Gray	Charles Main
Arthur Kennedy	Nellie Wood
Melvin Winters	Velma Amos
Emmet Chambers	Eliza Kennedy
Oakey Adams	Raymond Main
Clyde Shelton	Helen Wood
Roy Holmes	John Amos
Glenn Wood	

Chapter 11
Page 1 by Helen Winters Wilson
History of the One-Room School

From the very early days education was always on many educators' minds such as John McDowell who came over from Scotland. He came to West Finley to teach when the township was just a territory. He was succeeded by David Frazier, Alexander Burns, and Jonathan Parkinson. The early teaching was in the hones.

I would like to write some history on the beginning of the one-room schools here in Washington County. In the early days, West Finley, East Finley, Donegal, and other areas were called territories. One of the early teachers was William Alms.

A school teacher was paid by subscription, as was the case everywhere in western Pennsylvania. In the Finley area the subscription was generally paid in rye, which was taken to a distillery.

The locations of each school house in this part of Finley Township were known as Kimmins, Chase, Frazier's, McCoy's, Knob, Windy Gap, Good Intent, and Gunn.

The township in West Finley sent James Holmes to the county convention held in Washington November 4, 1834 for the purpose of deciding whether the county of Washington should accept the provisions of the act passed on April 4, 1834 providing for a general system of education throughout the state.

It was moved by William Patterson of Cross Creek Township that a tax (a levy) be placed into the operation of the law. This motion was seconded by Thomas Ringland of Morris Township. It carried twenty-one votes being cast in favor and five against it. The delegate from West Finley, James Holmes, voted yea.

At that time there were in West Finley Township two hundred and thirty-three persons libel to pay school tax and the portion of tax for the township was one hundred and ninety-one dollars and ninety-nine cents, which was raised. The next year there was an assessed levied, and the money collected for school purposes that year was two hundred, sixty-nine dollars and ninety-six cents.

The township was divided into school districts under the charge of J. Henderson and A. Powers, the school directors elected at the first election. The meeting was held October 14, 1834 at the home of John Daugherty; the president was John Sutherland.

School houses were soon erected in these districts and through the operation of the school law a cornerstone of education had begun for the education of our children.

The school report of 1863 showed there were in the township ten districts with ten schools, ten teachers, and 475 scholars.

In 1873 there were eleven districts, eleven schools, and 419 scholars enrolled. The amount of money received for school purposes at that time was $2,628.17.

In 1880 there were eleven districts, eleven schools, and 379 scholars enrolled. Time and experience modified its imperfections until the present successful method we have working in our schools today.

Chapter 12
Kimmins One-Room School No. 3
West Finley Township, Washington Co., PA

The Kimmins one-room school in the years of 1936 and 1937 presented an interesting time for the teacher Dorotha Montgomery who had recently finished her education and was ready to teach. Dorotha, who lived on West Finley Road not far from the school, drove her car, a black 1932 Chevrolet, and parked it in front of school.

I recently talked to Doris Chambers Smith who attended the Kimmins school in her first three years. She lived on Chambers Ridge Road and walked to school each day. Doris told me her mother Elda watched as I walked down the steep, scary hill to Marinda Gray's house and then I ran the short distance to the school house.

In 1936 Doris and Junior Main were in first grade. Doris's brother Arley started the next year for two years and in 1938 the one-room schools closed.

Some of the students were Glenn, Edward, Mary Jane & Evelyn Main, Jim & Albert Daugherty, Bob McClerry, Margaret King, Evelyn Hess, Mable, Ruth, Gladys & Charles Fry, Louise Stricklin, Roy, Ruth & Junior King.

Doris loved her little reading book where she studied the adventures of Dick, Jane, and Sally and her arithmetic where she learned her multiplication tablets. Dorotha taught me those tablets and I never forgot them; she was a wonderful teacher.

Dorotha gave stars and cards for spelling, the alphabet, and writing. In first grade we learned to print our name on the blackboard and learned to spell words. In second grade we got our own McGuffey primer and spelling book. Doris loved her primer.

There was no well at the school; a pipe came out of the ground. The water was from a spring close by. In winter, a bucket of water was carried in and set on a table in the back of the room. Bob McClerry and Charley Fry were in charge of that duty.

In the winter Jim and Albert Daugherty carried in the coal for the pot-bellied stove that sat in the middle row between our desks. Jim and Albert banked the stove each afternoon to try and keep it going during the week. Dorotha came early to get the stove going before we arrived, and she rang the first bell.

We all walked to school except Bob McClerry who rode his bike and parked it on the porch. One day Bob caught his foot in the spokes and cut his foot and Dorotha took him home during recess. We played fox and geese; we formed a large circle and the fox ran after the geese. No one wanted to be the fox.

In the winter months Doris had a navy blue snow suit that her mom bought her from the Sears Roebuck catalog. Her mother and grandma Martha designed a little outfit to wear to the Christmas party—a little plaid skirt and velvet yellow blouse.

For the Christmas party Dorotha brought oil lamps and set them along the side of the room, as the party was in the evening. There was a Christmas tree one of the boys brought from their farm, and it was decorated with bells and chains made of paper.

Junior and Doris were in first grade and shared the same wide desk and sat in the front row. At the Christmas party Doris and Junior sang "Twinkle Twinkle Little Star." Doris's mother brought fried chicken, chocolate cake, and delicious cinnamon buns. Dad Emmett, Mom Elda, and Grandma Martha along with brothers Arley and Kenny attended the party and were driven in their 1928 Chevrolet truck. Arley and Kenny loved to come to school and Kenny was just three at that Christmas party.

School was out the last week of April. The students and their parents enjoyed a picnic lunch. The parents brought potato salad, chicken sandwiches, and several cakes. Dorotha sent our grades and reports to the school board to be checked for graduation and promotion. Roy King and Ruth Frye graduated from eighth grade that spring. Doris and Junior were promoted to second grade that beautiful spring day in 1937.

Chapter 13
No. 2 School, Marshall Co., Dallas, WV

In the year 1936 a young girl started to school. Her name was Anna Patricia Wilson; she was just five years old. Her two older brothers Duane, nine, and Robert, seven, walked up a long lane to the ridge road that took them to school. Here is Patricia's story.

The three of us walked along a gravel road for a mile to reach the school, no matter the weather conditions. Some winter days were very difficult; I remember the winter of 1936 there was lots of snow. It snowed for several days; the drifts covered over fence posts and were very crusty. Duane and Robert went ahead and Robert took my hand as we climbed over the fence posts together. The snow was over top of my over shoes; and my stockings were all wet with snow. I also had on wool mittens and my hands were also getting very cold.

There was no transportation. Occasionally a neighbor would give us a ride on his horse or Dad would take us to school in our horse drawn sleigh. That was lots of fun!

My first-grade teacher was Homer Crow. In the center of the room was a pot-bellied stove fueled by coal and tended by Mr. Crow. In the vestibule we left our over shoes and dinner bucked. Our mother Anna always fixed us a wonderful lunch; her peanut butter and chicken sandwiches were always so good. And we always had a cookie and in fall when the grapes were ripe a pod of juicy grapes.

Learning my ABCs was a lot of fun and I soon learned to read out of the McGuffey primer. My school mates in first grade were Floyd Milliken and Charles Kiger.

I loved school; it was a wonderful experience. In the spring many of the parents came out for the last day of school. My mother Anna came bringing her baked beans and apple pie. My sister Catherine was three years old that April day. When Miss Jones handed me my report card in spring of 1940 I was promoted to sixth grade.

Certificates were handed out with our report card—how happy I was to see all A's on my card. For my perfect attendance in first grade I received a little cloth purse with a little leather handle. I loved that little purse. Mother put my first grade picture inside it and that little purse I kept for many years.

Harry Lydick was my second and third grade teacher. Mr. Lydick was very strict; he didn't put up with students who misbehaved. What I learned from him was to be quiet.

Throughout my next four years, my most memorable teacher was Miss Edna Jones. I was asked to help Charles with his penmanship. Writing was very important when we were in grade school; also she encouraged reading, art, music, and history.

Each year a school nurse would come out from Moundsville and give us a check-up to see if all students were vaccinated. All students entering the first grade had to be vaccinated against smallpox. I hated the little wooden tongue depressor she used to check our tonsils. I always tried to be at the end of the line.

A music teacher taught us several songs, usually songs like "God Bless America," many sad songs, "Two Little Orphans" and "Life Is Like a Mountain Railroad." Music time was always lots of fun. We had a piano though I don't remember who played it.

Recess was always a lot of fun. We played tag, musical chairs, and softball. Robert usually had a ball in his pocket, and we girls took turns swinging in air. When recess was over Miss Jones had a bell on her desk that she would ring.

A PTA meeting was held once a month so the parents and teachers could discuss their views and ask questions or make comments regarding the interest of all the children. The teacher usually went over some of their reading and spelling skills for each student. Mother always went to the meetings and that was when I found out how well I was doing in school. Our mother was always teaching us how to behave at school.

In 1938 a new family moved into the area by the name of Fonner; they had several boys—Norman, Martin, Herman, Fred, and their older brother Tom. The first day of school the boys all came to school with white shirts on.

Each year the school floor was oiled to keep down the dust. I don't remember who started the wrestling match with those little boys, but Miss Jones was needed to break up the match. I don't remember who won! It was an unexpected event!

Our Christmas party was one of the big events just before Christmas. At the party when I was in fifth grade, Catherine and I sang "Santa Clause Is Coming to Town." Santa Claus came through the door with his bells on and his hoho voice. We all had to tell him what we wanted for Christmas. For me he said, "You have been a good little girl, Patty." He reached into his sack and handed me a little box of candy.

Miss Jones took me to Moundsville to see the movie *Bambi.* That was the first movie I ever saw. During my last year in grade school there was a golden horseshoe test on what we had learned about the state of West Virginia. Miss Jones took me to Moundsville to take the test. I didn't win but it was such a learning experience I never forgot.

As me, my brothers Duane and Robert, and sister Catherine walked down that old stone road to study in that old one-room school long ago, we all turned out really well. I worked and raised my three children while working sterilizing medical and surgical supplies at Wheeling Hospital. Duane worked for the gas company. Robert was in the Korean

War and worked for B&O and C&O Railroad as one of their officers. Catherine raised her four children and is enjoying her retirement.

Some school mates were Lucille Murphy, Jean Gettings, cousin Bernadine Riggle, Robert, Duane, and Catherine. Our walk to school each day was always the highlight of my day, and I have many memories I will never forget.

Chapter 14
No. Two One-Room School
Marshall Co., Dallas, WV

In the year 1934 a little boy who was just five years old started to school at the No. 2 one-room school. His name was Robert Elmer Wilson. He was enrolled in primer class and his teacher that year was Nora Harsh. Here is his story.

I had an older brother Duane, so starting to school was no problem. Miss Harsh was very interested in me; she had me seated near her desk as I was the only student in her primer class. She taught me my ABCs using the McGuffey spelling book.

Morning exercises were always started with roll call and each student stood up and told the class their name. We were assigned seats according to our year in school. Duane sat across from me and having him close was very helpful.

Miss Harsh had us stand and recite the Pledge of Allegiance and Lord's Prayer each Monday morning. Every Tuesday we learned a new verse from the Bible.

In fall just before school started Louis Potts brought school supplies. Each student was given a tablet and pencil for writing. There was chalk, erasers, two brooms, and writing paper for the teacher. Our tablet and pencil had to last us till the next semester. We had an ink well on our desk and we learned to write with a ink pen. Writing was interesting and it was a class I really enjoyed.

In second and third grade I had Homer Crow. Mr. Crow was interested in reading. I picked up reading really fast. He had pictures with different stories that were in our reading book. I learned to read very well by the time I was in third grade and reading was a subject I really enjoyed. My reading skills helped me master many problems in my lifetime. He instructed spelling and we had spelling tests every Friday, which were usually done on the blackboard. I never had any trouble with spelling as it always took me to another interesting word.

My fourth and fifth grade teacher was Harry Lydick. Mr. Lydick arrived each morning on his horse that he tied to a post behind the coal shed. He taught by the hickory stick and his teachings were by description and correction.

One day he brought several little fish to school in a cup of water. When he dropped them in a glass of milk they lived but when he dropped them in a cup of coffee they died. That was one lesson I learned in his class, and his lessons were mostly by example.

For our Thanksgiving play while I was in fifth grade he cut one of the brooms to make a crutch for Charles's part in the play. One of the girls was sweeping with the second broom and broke the handle.

Mr. Lydick was very upset about the broom handle being broken. He asked us five boys Duane, George, Danny, Charles, and myself if we broke the broom handle and we all answered no.

While holding the remaining part of the broom handle in his hand, he said, "I'm going to give each one of you boys a licking. Then I will get the right one." He got the Bible out of the desk and said, "Though shall not lie."

This got to be too much for the girls and Evelyn confessed she broke the handle of the broom while sweeping the floor. Mr. Lydick said, "I'm going to give you one lick for each one of the boys." After that incident, we were all very upset.

When we went home and told our parents what had happened our parents all got involved. This called for a special meeting held Friday evening at the school house.

Elizabeth Riggle who was in charge of the meeting stood up on the rostrum and said, "Mr. Lydick, we as parents will not accept this kind of behavior with our children."

When the meeting was over my dad Luther took Mr. Lydick by the shirt collar and said, "Mr. Lydick, don't you ever pull that trick again; if my boys need a licking, I will take care of that problem when they come home." My dad was very upset by the way Mr. Lydick was teaching the children and dismissal plans were discussed. A letter was sent to the Marshall County school office to have Mr. Lydick dismissed.

One morning Mr. Lydick was late getting to school and came in with blood all over the front of his shirt. On the way to school that morning Mr. Lydick was confronted by Mr. Coldwell who met him along the road. This concerned his daughter Helen whom Mr. Lydick had failed in school. All the students were very upset that morning.

Just before Christmas we boys Duane, Danny, and I would be excused in the afternoon to go to the woods and pick out a hemlock tree to be decorated for our Christmas party. We were always looking to find at least a five-foot tree and Miss Jones helped several of the girls with the decorations.

My last two years at school Edna Jones was my teacher; she enjoyed her job and was very concerned about all the students. We had spelling bees often and I always was able to stand up among the last two students, when Miss Jones asked me to spell chauffeur. I never spelled it wrong again.

We had a box social and the girls would bring pretty decorated boxes filled with good things to eat. There was an auctioneer who would come to school and auction each box to the highest bidder. I bought the box that my mother Anna brought and I enjoyed eating with her the chicken sandwich and chocolate cupcake she had prepared.

In spring just before school was out a big home coming was held; students and their parents from nearby schools would come to the big event. There was a lot of good food and several big watermelons were cut and passed around just before closing. Another school year had ended and I graduated from eighth grade in 1943 and moved to Sherrard High School. Mr. Lydick was my homeroom teacher.

As Mr. Lydick was dismissed from the No. 2 school, having problems with all the children who lived there, many students were afraid to ask to be excused to go to the restroom. Patty was afraid to say anything in his class.

One day just before report cards came out he told me he was going to fail me in my agriculture class. Can you imagine a teacher telling a student that information? I went to my locker after the reports came out, got my personal things, and went home. Several boys from our area also quit school at that time.

I got a landscaping job that summer. I walked over a mile and caught a ride with our neighbor Douey. I worked at the landscaping job until I was drafted into the Korean War in 1952.

I served in the Korean War for two years as a tank commander and was discharged in April 1954. During that time I was engaged to my wife Helen and we were married that spring on June 5th.

In my life I always tried to work my way up in any job I was lucky enough to obtain. I got a job with the railroad in the Brotherhood of Maintenance of Way Department as vice chairman where I had my own car representing the railroad employees. I retired in the spring of 1990.

Robert Elmer Wilson, age 12, 1942

Chapter 15
No. 2 One-Room School
Marshall Co., Dallas, WV

In the year 1915 Elmer Wilson was president of all the public schools in Marshall County District No. 2. The secretary was Frank Kimmins, and other board members were William Dague, Charles Howard, and A. M. McCausland. The superintendent was H. W. McDowell and the teacher Anna Atkinson.

President Elmer Wilson visited the school often checking with Miss Atkinson on the progress of each student. Each student was assigned a McGuffey primer. The students learned to recognize a word by a picture. Miss Atkinson was instructed to pursue the phonic method, word method, alphabet method, or a combination of the three in her teachings.

In 1915 there were thirty-eight students enrolled. Miss Atkinson assigned several students duties during the school year. Alda, an eighth grade student, helped the teacher work with the young students with their spelling, while they were preparing for a spelling bee with other local schools. Alta McCausland won the spelling bee with the older children and Regenia Marshall with the younger group. On the way home from Dallas, while sitting in a sleigh driven by William Dague, they sang "School Days." For good behavior, Miss Atkinson gave each student a pencil.

Harry, Russell, and Elmer Jackson raised sugar cane on their farm and were always telling stories about making syrup out of the cane. They had a mill that was run by a team of horses; the horses walked around in circles squeezing out the syrup, which was heated and used as molasses.

Geneva, Velma, and Lillian Riggle walked over a mile to school; if it was raining or cold their dad brought them in a buggy. We walked up a long hill through the woods and sometimes we got really cold. During the winter months we wore long wool stockings, wool mittens, and a toboggan pulled down over our ears. Sometimes dad let Lillian drive the horse and we always had lots of fun singing as we rode along.

Luther Wilson and Cecil Dague loved to play baseball and Luther carried a ball to school in his lunch pail. After lunch the ball game began with Clyde Ruffle who always had his bat ready as the bat was always kept at school. Other players were Venard and Arthur Marshall, Harold Nuss, Bernard Gittings, and Curtis Howard. Other schools we played were Upper Sand Hill, Oak Hill, and Dallas. The games were held on Saturday and we got together and walked to games.

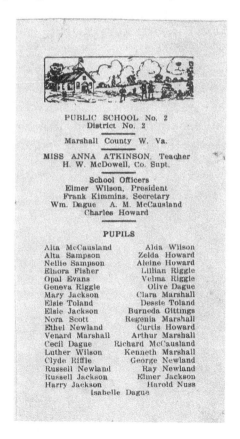

PUBLIC SCHOOL No. 2
District No. 2

Marshall County W. Va.

MISS ANNA ATKINSON, Teacher
H. W. McDowell, Co. Supt.

School Officers
Elmer Wilson, President
Frank Kimmins, Secretary
Wm. Dague   A. M. McCausland
Charles Howard

PUPILS

Alta McCausland	Alda Wilson
Alta Sampson	Zelda Howard
Nellie Sampson	Alcine Howard
Elnora Fisher	Lillian Riggle
Opal Evans	Velma Riggle
Geneva Riggle	Olive Dague
Mary Jackson	Clara Marshall
Elsie Toland	Dessie Toland
Elsie Jackson	Burneda Gittings
Nora Scott	Regenia Marshall
Ethel Newland	Curtis Howard
Venard Marshall	Arthur Marshall
Cecil Dague	Richard McCausland
Luther Wilson	Kenneth Marshall
Clyde Riffle	George Newland
Russell Newland	Ray Newland
Russell Jackson	Elmer Jackson
Harry Jackson	Harold Nuss
Isabelle Dague	

Alda Wilson was preparing to become a teacher and that was on her mind most of the time. He mother Pearl wanted her only daughter to become a teacher. On their farm, on No. 2 Ridge Road near Dallas, the family had two gas wells. Alta's father Elmer had a large business with chickens; he sold baby chicks and eggs—a big business in those days. The baby chicks were five cents each and eggs were fifty cents a dozen. Elmer Wilson was a very prosperous man when he lost his life in 1926 and left his son Luther in charge of their large farm.

Upon graduation from school Alta went to West Liberty College to finish her education as a teacher. She married John Francis and became a mother of five children—Clyde, Clara Pearl, Joyce, George, and Janet.

In 1926 Luther married Anna Toland and they are the parents of five children—Duane, Robert, Patty, Catherine, and Mary Ellen.

On the last day of school in 1916, Elmer Wilson was at the school for the closing ceremony. Isabelle Dague, Alta Sampson, and Alda Wilson received their eighth grade diplomas. Isabelle received a certificate for perfect attendance. Elmer told the students that "Friendship formed in your childhood becomes the genies that rule your life."

Chapter 16
No. 2 One-Room School
Marshall Co., Dallas, WV

In the year 1946 Lenora Harsh was teaching at the school and there were eighteen students enrolled. Miss Harsh lived close and usually walked the short distance each morning and rang the eight AM bell for the children to report to school.

This school was one of the twelve schools in the Sand Hill district and was the second free school built in the district, which is how it got its name No. 2. The first school was built at Dallas in 1870 by James Amos and John Creighton.

The first teacher was Ferdinand Stricklin, and Ann Roney was the first to end the school term with a big basket dinner. The parents and all the community came out to that special event. Several of the boys—Herman, Fred, and Marvin Fonner—brought their ball and bat and played ball in the backyard. In the afternoon the children were treated to ice cream and watermelon.

In 1901 a new school house was built on the old foundation. The school term was seven months and the parents bought the children their books. There were not many books to go around and several families shared what books they had.

Shirley Riggle and Ruby Huff were in second grade; Betty Huff and Marvin Fonner third grade; Catherine Wilson and Frank Riggle seventh grade; Sylvia Huff and Jenny Jackson first grade; and Russell Riggle was in eighth grade.

In the spring of 1955 the school closed along with the county schools in Marshall County, WV, and the students were bussed to the Sand Hill school near Dallas.

Front row: Sylvia Huff, Jenny Jackson, Shirley Riggle, Ruby and Betty Huff, Marvin Fonner, Howard Daugherty. Second row: George Kitchen, Charles Stine. Third row: Frank Sayer, Eula Jean Riggle, Herman Fonner, Russell Riggle, Catherine Wilson, Frank Stein, Fred Fonner, Ed Atwell, and Frank Riggle.

Chapter 17
Oak Hill School, Sand Hill, WV

In 1906, Elmer Merinar was the teacher at the Oak Hill one-room school in Sand Hill, WV. It was his first year of teaching.

The school was known as Oak Hill because it was located on a hill with oak trees that surrounded it at one time. The school was built on land donated by the Sheet family.

The school house was an ordinary log cabin with a large fireplace on one end. The floor seats were made by splitting small trees into two parts, hewing the flat side smooth installing legs and making a bench without a back.

The bench was hewed very smooth and set on pegs along the wall to make a writing desk. The rooms were often lit by cutting sections of the logs out and covering the opening with greased paper. The room was heated by a fireplace.

There was an abundance of wood as many of the early schools were built in woods or at the side of the road. Many of the young men were familiar with using an ax.

Later a hewed log house was built with a floor of sawed planks fit together with seats made of boards with a back on them and board wall for writing. Our early ancestors discovered that they could paint a board black and have a blackboard. A stove in the center of the room for wood or coal for heating took the place of cabins long ago.

Some of the early teachers were Sherman Welch, Alice Dague, Blanch Merinar, Louis Dague Hill, Clara Pearl Wilson Folmar, Mable Gray, and Ethel Armstrong. Marjorie Dague Stedman was the last teacher to teach at this school. The school closed in 1939 and the students were assigned to Brett Run School.

Spelling was carefully studied and many lessons were taught by the rule of a hickory stick. Students were taught respect and to be polite to each other.

Gertrude White was born January 27, 1893 and was thirteen in 1906 and was in seventh grade at Oak Hill. She was very talented and played the harmonica. Gertrude loved to play for school activities and at the Christmas program she played "Jingle Bells" and "Here Comes Santa Claus" just before Santa arrived through the door.

At the Easter program she played "The Easter Parade" while Rose and Ethel Sheets sang the lyrics to the song. Gertrude played at the local Methodist church for many occasions.

Their were several Sheet students Lilly (first grade), James (second), and Oscar (fourth). Rose was in seventh grade along with her friend Anna Steinman. George Merinar who was Elmer's father assisted the younger students when they needed help.

Clara Pearl Wilson Folmar taught at the school in 1937 after graduating from West Liberty College. Some of her duties were the school nurse and janitor. She kept a bottle of aspirin in her purse and assigned one of the students to sweep the floor.

In 1938 for Easter Clara Pearl stopped at Murphys Five and Ten and bought the students a small straw basket and filled it with a package of jelly beans.

When the final reports were handed out on April 27th, Jenny Homes had perfect attendance and Mary Riggs had all A's on her report card. Mary, who was in sixth grade, walked up to Clara Pearl and gave her a hug. She asked all the students what they wanted to be when they grew up. Mary said she wanted to be a school teacher.

On the last day of school a large picnic lunch was held and they all came out with their basket filled with goodies. Opal Dague's mother brought chocolate cupcakes. The graduation class was Jane Winters and John Lilly. Clara Pearl pinned a rose on Jane's dress, as she was an honor student. Clara Pearl then transferred to the Viola one-room school in West Virginia.

Food note: Clara Pearl Wilson Folmar was 101 when she died in January 28, 2019.

Chapter 18
Cooneytown School, West Finley Township, Washington Co., PA

The school was a short distance from the little town of Beham and was located on Ridge Road that leads towards the West Virginia state line. The school was built on the Dague family farm and was located just above the barn where cattle grazed each summer.

There was never a large number of students enrolled at Coonytown, as the area was back in the country on a dirt road. The children walked to school or were driven to school in a buggy and in winter months they had lots of fun with a horse and sleigh.

In 1903 there were fourteen students enrolled during the school year and their teacher was Fern Travis who came to school on her horse and was seated side saddle. She tied her horse that she called Bell to a hitching post in front of the school.

Mary Little, who was born November 22, 1886, and Olive Gunn were in eighth grade. The picture was taken by a photographer from Wheeling who came around each year and took pictures of students.

Most of their writing was done on a slate with white chalk. Students learned to read in Dick and Jane readers and the alphabet was taught from the McGuffey spelling book.

Mary had good grades and her plans were to become a teacher. Her brother Lynn would be taking her to Claysville Teachers Institute to study in the fall. When the weather was nice outside Lynn drove her to Claysville in a buggy. During the winter months she completed most of her studies at home.

First Row: Earl Dague second from left and Alice Armstrong first girl from left. Alice's sister is holding the slate and the Trussel children are standing on the right.

When school was out on April 21, 1903 many of the young men had no way of getting around, as transportation by car was almost never heard of in those days. Owning a Model Tee Ford was only a dream and many of the young men stayed on the farm. Several found work at gas pumping stations or they would go into town looking for whatever work they could find.

Earl Dague, who was in fifth grade, chose to stay on the farm when he graduated and maybe get work at Magersville gas pumping station or help his dad on the farm. Earl was very good at arithmetic and could recite his multiplication tables and new most of the measure and metric system. Earl was promoted to sixth grade that fall.

Nellie Wallace, who was in seventh grade, was the only student who had perfect attendance. Nellie wanted to be a teacher as Miss Travis talked to all the girls about teaching. Around 1903 when Mary and Olive graduated from eighth grade, teaching was not thought about by many of the younger children as they had no way to travel and many of the girls just stayed at home and got married.

At the turn of the century, travel was one big problem. Even if a student wanted to go anywhere there was no transportation. If you were born in the country, many times that was where you ended up. Many of the young men would walk several miles to catch a ride with anyone who was going into town. One young man named Robert walked seven miles one summer to catch a ride to his landscaping job and saved enough money to purchase his first car, a second-hand Chevrolet.

Chapter 19
Gunn School, West Finley Township, Washington Co., PA

The Gunn school was located in West Finley on West Finley Road about four miles from the little village of Burnesville. The Gunn school (the building still stands today) was located on Alexander Gunn's large farm. The Gunn family were pioneers of Washington County. Alexander's brother Franklin died May 27, 1907 at his home, the oldest man of Washington County at the age of ninety-two.

Children attending the school were Hartzell, Horr, Galentine, Carson, Ewing, Richey, Scherich, and Coldwell. The population consisted mainly of farmers and gas company workers.

In the year 1919, there were sixteen students enrolled at school and the teacher was Lillian Montgomery. Most of the children walked to school. The Montgomery family had a 1914 Chevrolet, and their dad brought the two girls Leah and Dorotha to school each day. Gye worked for the gas company in Majorsville and dropped the girls off on his way to work.

Ola and Emmett Carson lived close to school. Emmett was assigned to bring in the water from the dug well each morning. The bucket sat near the teacher's desk. Each student had their own folded cups. Emmett and Ralph Caldwell brought in the coal for the stove that sat in the middle of the room. In winter months Emmett attended the stove.

The English alphabet, consisting of twenty-six letters, is divided into vowels and consonants. The teacher taught the vowels with a song, a, e, i, o, u, w, and y. Dorothy grew up to become a teacher in the one-room schools. Edith Horr married Glenn Ewing. Ola Carson married Ralph Hartzell.

There was five Coldwell children—Dorothy, Freda, Joseph, Ralph, and Delphia. At the Easter party Freda sang, "The Easter Parade." Bessie Horr had perfect attendance that year and she said, "that she wouldn't miss school for anything."

The Halloween party was held on October 31, 1915 and all the children dressed up in their costumes. Dorothy was the cutest dressed as Cinderella; Emmett Carson was dressed like a farmer. Ralph brought a large tub and the older students bobbed for apples. The teacher had popcorn growing in her garden and made popcorn balls. She also gave the students a small bag of candy corn to take home.

The Christmas party was held just before Christmas vacation. Bertha Horr, who was in eighth grade, helped the teacher with the Christmas party. They decided to exchange names so each student would get a gift that would not cost more than fifty cents. The teacher gave each student a box of crayons.

Glenn Horr and his sister Bessie had transferred from the Knob school the year before and moved closer to the Gunn school area. On the property where the Horr family lived there were several blue spruce trees. Miss Montgomery sent Glenn and Ralph to the woods and they brought back a six-foot tree. Bessie and Edith decorated the tree with paper bells and strings of icicles made with gold paper.

Betty Caldwell brought a gallon of apple cider and Mrs. Carson made cupcakes. Bertha handed out the gifts; Dorothy and Freda each got a small doll, several of the children got gloves. Dorotha and Edith each got the book, *Little Women*. Everyone was waiting for Santa Claus who came through the door jingling his bells with his ho, ho and his red sack flung over his back filled with candy for all the children who attended the Christmas party at the Gunn school in 1919.

The Gunn school in 1918. To the right is a dug well and the Alexander Gunn apple orchard.

Chapter 20
Stoney Point School, East Finley Township, Washington Co., PA

Stoney School got its name from the stoney area the school was built on. Stoney was located in the center of the township. Most of the school's business meetings were held at Stoney. The school was located on East Finley Drive.

Shirley Clutter Plants attended the Stoney school through seventh grade then her family moved from Enon Valley to Claysville where she graduated from high school.

Shirley's parents were Havel and Sarah Margaret Clutter; her brothers Stanley and Earl Clutter were also students at the school.

Some of Shirley's school mates were Jean Carter, Edna Shape, Joan Brownlee, Betty Filby, Ralph Shaw, and Shirley's cousin Lena Clutter.

Teachers were Harry Carter, Harry Allen, and Zoe Carter. Bus drivers were Harry Workman, Wilbert Ealy, and Harry Thompson.

Ruby Jones had polio and Harry Thompson transported her and her sister Mildred and brother Clayton to school in his 1941 Chevrolet.

In first grade Shirley's teacher was Zoe Carter. One afternoon Shirley turned around in her seat to see what the commotion was in back of school and Miss Carter pulled her hair. She never forgot that instant teaching example and she never will.

On Valentine's Day we each had our own shoe box decorated with crepe paper. Miss Carter gave each one of us a small box of candy hearts. Ralph Shaw gave me a card with a pink rose on top with small drops of morning dew. That was one of my favorite valentine cards. I made most of my valentines and several of students bought their valentines at Clover farm store in Claysville.

I had a little red lunch pail and mother made the best tasting bread and cinnamon buns. She would prepare our lunch with peanut butter and jelly sandwiches and maybe a cupcake, cookie, or an apple. We had our little folding cups for drinking.

We played games such as fox and geese at recess and after lunch (no one ever wanted to be the fox). We also played jacks, marbles, and jumped rope till Miss Carter rang the bell that called us back into school after lunch.

In fall of 1931 an American flag was bought by the school board for all the schools in East Finley. Teachers were hired at the board meeting in April. Their salary was based on the amount of education each teacher had.

During the Great Depression year 1945, when the war was going on, there was a shortage of parachutes and many school children were asked to collect the milkweed pods that were used in making parachutes. In fall after we had started back school and the pods of milkweed plants were at their best, my brothers Stanley, Earl, and I took paper flour sacks and went to the neighbor's pasture to pick milkweed pods one September afternoon in 1945.

William Holmes McGuffey early school books were used at that time by all the schools. There were three books—arithmetic, spelling, and primer—for the first-grade students. McGuffey taught by the rule of alphabet, reading, writing, and arithmetic. McGuffey's theory was for each student to have good reading skills. The books for younger children were small so little hands could hold them.

In 1930 the Peterson handwriting was taught at all schools. Mr. Rhinehart was the instructor. He was paid $25 dollars a month, five days a week for four months. The Peterson writing included posture, sitting up straight with your arm on the desk. On a lined piece of paper the students were instructed to practice slanting, up, down, ovals, and circles. Mr. Rhinehart's sayings was "Round, round, ready, write."

Chapter 21
Dickerson School, South Franklin Township, Washington Co., PA

The Dickerson one-room school building sat about one and a quarter mile south of Hathaway store on Route 221. The red brick building was about fifty feet from the road.

Mary Jane Chase Sprowls attended the Dickerson school through sixth grade along with her six siblings—Alma, Frank, Bill, Charles, Harry, and Ellis.

Mary started to school in the fall of 1921 and her teacher was Mary Pancost. Her best friend at Dickerson was Ruth Hartley. The teachers were Anna Woodburn, Opal Ryan, Ramson Day, and Albert Strawn. The Dickerson school closed in 1960, and Mary Coal was the last teacher who taught there.

Some of the interesting things Mary remembers about the building was the blackboard that extended three fourths of the way across the upper side of the room. The platform was the same length. On a shelf inside the door sat the water cooler with a spigot attached at the bottom.

As you entered the school, to the left of the door a rope hung through the ceiling. The rope was attached to a bell that hung in the belfry on top of the roof. In the front lower corner was a cupboard with several shelves where we placed our lunch pails.

In the ceiling were narrow, grooved boards painted gray. The windows had light-colored window blinds. In the center of the room sat the pot-bellied coal stove. The pupil's desk had a seat attached in front and a seat size was based on the student's grade level.

The oil lamps were attached to a wrought iron holder that was attached to the wall. The teachers would board with a family who lived close to the school; there they received their meals and a place to sleep. Very few teachers lived close to a school. The teachers had no way to travel; there were very few cars in those days.

There was a large playground and many happy hours were spent playing there. One of my favorite games was Blackman—a tag game with bases. In winter after it had snowed we made a large circle with a cross in the center and played fox and geese.

Another game we played was run, sheep, run. Several of us would go and hide in the field and another bunch would hunt us. The first group that got to home base was the winner. I remember Hazel Hathaway went sliding on her butt on the cement porch. I'm sure she must remember that incident better than I. Ellis was standing close by and came to her rescue.

There was a spring below the big oak tree that stood out back of the school. At recess, Hazel, Frank, and I used to run down to the spring to quench our thirst. Later there was a well drilled at the sight. The small children always needed assistance at the pump as the pump handle was hard for them to handle.

Many times Frank and I would race home trying to see which one of us could make it home in the fastest time. Frank raced very fast; many times he would make it home first. I will never forget that time I beat Frank to the back door.

Wilbert Strawn told me how my brother Frank would bring a dill pickle in his lunch pail and he would trade the pickle to Wilbert for chocolate lunch cake.

Mary remembers the day her mother died—December 8, 1925. We lived at Doc. Charles Cracraft home at the time. Opal Ryan was the teacher and she brought all the students to our home that day. I remember seeing them walking down the road. I was just nine years old and was in fourth grade. That was a very sad day for all us children; Charles, Harry, and Ellis were much younger. We took care of one another and I was always the older girl who helped raise my brothers. My sister Alma was always there to help in the kitchen, and she baked Harold and I our wedding cake in 1936.

One funny incident took place during my happy times at Dickerson. My friend Ruth Hartley and I had to stay after school one afternoon to get our reading assignment. The story we were assigned to was soap-making. As I was reading along thinking I was doing very well, I came to the place where they cooked the soap in large vats and I said they cooked the *soup* in a very large vat. The teacher, Ruth, and I got very tickled over that little incident and it turned out to be funny and a very happy memory.

Mont Auld owned the first school bus in our community, which was a horse-drawn spring wagon and surrey. In those days students were bussed to the Bethel school so the school would have enough students to keep it open.

Charlie Bryner along with his siblings walked to Dickerson. They lived one and six-tenths mile away. Their father was paid twenty-five dollars a year, per child, for them to walk the distance. The law required students to walk if they lived one-and-a-half mile from school; if the distance was farther the family was paid the fee.

Mary was a good student at Dickerson and kept a record of her grades when she was in fourth grade. Her grades were reading 91, writing 82, spelling 90, language 86, and arithmetic 82. She was promoted to fifth grade by her teacher Opal Ryan.

Harold Sprowls and I were wed on April 20, 1936 in Wheeling, WV. A friend loaned us six dollars to make the trip to Wheeling to get married. We were married sixty-three years when Harold died July 25, 1999 age eighty-four.

We were the parents of five children. Betty Ann, Charles, and John are deceased. Larry lives in Georgia, and Sue resides in Shenandoah, VA, where I make my home. I am 104 years old and enjoy writing, working in the flower garden, and traveling. When God calls me home, I will be ready. I thank God every day for my wonderful life I had with Harold who was always at my side helping me in our walk through life with our five children.

The Road Side Chapel is located on Chapel Hill Road off Burnesville Ridge Road north of Claysville, PA, and everyone is welcome to visit the chapel anytime.

Mary has lived close to God all her life and one evening while praying God appeared to her. In that vision she received a calling from God to build a place of worship.

Mary asked her nephew Darold Sprowls to take invitations to neighborhood children to come the following Sunday morning for worship in their basement. The first Sunday seven children came to worship; the following Sunday twenty-one children attended worship service. Plans to build the Road Side Chapel soon took place in the basement of their home.

The church began to grow in attendance and soon a larger building was needed for church service Mary and Harold donated part of their farm to build the chapel.

On July 22, 1967 the chapel was dedicated with a very large crowd of members and friends. Mary and Harold spoke at the dedication thanking members and friends who helped build the chapel. Among many of the guests were Doc Harry Hutchison and his wife Susanna. Doc Hutchison was a well-known doctor in the area.

On September 27, 2018 Mary, a talented writer, was 102 years old. Mary has written many stories and articles and is presently writing for *Small Town News* in Claysville, PA.

While writing these stories for *One-Room Schools in Past* Mary had the opportunity to meet many wonderful, talented people who shared their interesting stories of when they were students at many of the one-room schools of long ago.

Rev. Mary Sprowls, Harold and daughter Sue at the Road Side Chapel

Chapter 22
Lindley School, South Franklin Township, Washington Co., PA

The Lindley school was located on Route 221 about one-and-a-half mile northeast of Prosperity. It was about three yards from our home. Some years there wasn't enough children in our area to have school so we had to go to the Dickerson school, which was on Route 221 about four miles northwest of Prosperity.

For several years Mout Auld was paid fifty dollars to haul us in his two-horse surrey. Other years Dad received twenty-five dollars for each of us to walk to school.

We walked in all kinds of weather with nothing on our feet but socks and leather shoes treated with sheep tallow. Many times we walked in snow above our shoe tops.

In 1994 Robert W. Bryner was ninety-four and he said, "Walking hasn't killed me yet; I plan on living to be one hundred or die trying."

Their were thirty to thirty-five students who attended the Dickerson school. In any school year there was never more than twelve students attending the Lindley school.

At the top of the school a large bell twenty inches in dimension hung in the belfry. When the bell rang the children knew it was time to go to school. The first bell rang at 8:30 AM and the last bell rang at 9:00 AM. If you were not in your seat when the roll was called you were counted absent and an excuse from home was in order.

Every Monday when school took up we would say a verse from the Bible. "Jesus Wept" St. John 11:35 was used quite often. The teacher would lead us in the Lord's Prayer as we all bowed our heads. Each morning our small group of students would answer "present" as Miss Sanders called the roll. I came to school early as I wanted to be in my seat when the roll was called. One time when I was absent I had to take an excuse saying that I had a toothache. Charley skipped school one day and he got in trouble with Miss Sanders who would not put up with such nonsense.

The teacher didn't teach by lecture. Instead, Miss Sanders gave assignments for each of our subjects one day and the next day we either answered the questions orally or wrote the answers on the blackboard.

For reading, spelling, geography, and history we would go up to the platform. For arithmetic, writing, and grammar we wrote the problems on the blackboard.

When I was in fifth grade, George J. Woodburn had three or four hickory switches lying on top of the organ, up front. Mr. Woorburn knew how to use them and boy did they sting. If you didn't have your multiplication tablets ready on Friday you got a swat from behind. They were drilled into each student's mind. When you left fifth grade you were required to know your tablets.

At 10:30 we had a fifteen-minute recess. At the end of recess one ding of the bell and we were expected to go to our seats. Lunch was 12:00 to 1:00 PM and we all brought our lunch.

Following lunch was playtime. We would hurry and eat our lunch and get whatever game we were going to play started. Whether it was baseball, ante over the school house, sock and take it, fox and geese, catchers, go sheep go, or prisoner's base, we were always ready for exercise, and playing games was always lots of fun.

We always played what we called "shinny." We used a tin can for the puck and a stick that had a crook on the end like a hockey stick. I remember Eugene fastened a metal ring on the end of a broom handle for his shinny club.

We were having a pretty hot game one day and Charley got hit above the eye with his stick. Miss Sanders came out and said, "You boys throw away your sticks; there will be no more shinny games." Charley got a shiner out of that game. Siles Ross wanted to keep playing and he got mad and threw his stick over in the weeds. We started laughing and Miss Sanders told us that it was no laughing matter.

To get water at Lindley, Charley and I would take a large bucket and run up to our home and dip the bucket into our spring. Then we carried water back to school. In the bucket was a large dipper with a long handle and we kids took turns drinking from the dipper and putting it back in the bucket. Our home was about five hundred yards from school.

When the bell rang for our last recess at 2:15, we kids would make a bee-line either for the spring or toilet. School let out at 4:00 PM. We could not wait to get home.

We made our baseballs by unraveling old socks and wrapping the yarn into a ball; then we sowed the balls together with heavy black thread. What baseballs we had!

When the weather got cold, we would go to big woods after lunch. Several large oak trees stood near our school and it was a great place for us boys to explore.

One day while exploring we found a big hornet nest. Eugene and I got it down and took it into school. We were kids and didn't realize the trouble we were getting into.

It was really cold one morning and the pot-bellied stove was getting really hot. Several younger kids were sitting close to the stove to keep warm. All at once the hornets began to fly around the room and Naomi Mason started to cry. Maty Quene got scared and ran out the door screaming for help. My mother came down and helped us kids get the hornets out the door. The subject for the day was the hornets nest!

We played prisoner base after school and it would get a little rough sometimes. While playing the game one afternoon Okie Caldwell broke his leg while running from second to home base. That was the end of the prisoner base game.

In 1915 at the Dickerson school, Rev. Longhner visited the school and gave each one of us kids a little red Testament book. Rev. Longhner was the pastor at the Bethel Presbyterian Church on Route 18 near Prosperity.

For entertainment and school raising events it was a chance for the young people to get together. There was pie and box socials during the school year. The pie and boxes were prepared by the girls and women of the community.

The auctioneer was Frank Auld's dad Mout; he was lots of fun and he liked us kids. We all tried to get the teachers box and would bid it up quite high. The girls and the women of the community would bring pretty boxes all decorated in crepe paper and several boxes had big bows tied around them. Mr. Auld set the boxes with the bows attached back to be auctioned last. My dad gave Charley and I each two dollars as he knew the social was for a good cause. I bid my two dollars on Clara Manson's box; her chocolate nut candy she made was all wrapped up in wax paper. The money from the social was used to help buy reading books for the Lindley and Dickerson schools.

The last day of school was always a big day. I graduated from eighth grade in 1919. I still remember Miss Sanders handing me my diploma. There were only two of us graduating that year—Eugene Newland and myself. Frank Auld was in third grade when he walked up the isle that day in 1919 to get his report card. Frank was one happy kid when he looked at his card and saw that he would be in fourth grade.

On the last day of school Clara Mason and her little sister Naomi stood upon the platform and sang "School Days" while we all joined in.

School days, school days
Dear old golden rule days
Reading, writing, & arithmetic
Taught by the rule of the hickory stick
You were my sweet in calico
I was your bashful barefoot bow
You wrote on my slate, "I love you so"
When we were a couple of kids

Chapter 23
Acton Corner, York Co., Acton, ME

The School was located in Acton, Maine in York County. There were three one-room schools in Acton and Robert B. Williams attended the Acton Corner school. Here is his story.

On September 5, 1949, I was six and Mrs. Dunnell was my teacher during my time at Acton Corner. She lived across the road from the school with her husband.

During the winter months of 1949 there was a lot of snow. The snow piled up in big drifts and Acton Corner would be closed sometimes several days at time. During that time my mother read me stories from the McGuffey Reader and had me recite my ABCs every day. My mother taught me morals, to say thank you and please, and to have good behavior, which I have tried to do all my life.

My mother made my lunch every day. I had a Mickey Mouse lunch pail that I loved to carry to school. My friend Dave was always asking me what I had in my pail. One day my mother put a Milky Way candy bar in my lunch and I shared it with Dave.

Mrs. Dunnell reminded us kids Thursday afternoon just before the last bell rang to bring a bowl and spoon with us Friday morning. She would go to her home across the road and bring back a big pot of soup that she had prepared that morning and a box of saltine crackers. On a cold day her tomato soup tasted so good.

Mrs. Dunnell and her husband had several goats that sometimes would escape from the fenced-in area. There would be at least two goats come running up the schoolhouse steps through the door and into the classroom.

They seemed to know where Mrs. Dunnell was. Several of the girls would scream and climb onto their desks. The older boys drove the goats out the door. They found the place where the goats crawled under the fence and drove them back into the pen.

Recess was a "fun time." The older kids would play baseball and horseshoe while the rest of us would play hide and seek, tag, red light, and giant steps.

Sometimes a boy would have to stay inside during recess; most of the time it was because of fighting and sometimes she would hear him swear. She would correct anyone who was using bad language. She was a Christian and if she heard a student use bad language she would ask them if they went to church.

I stayed in just one time. I was in third grade and I was out behind the schoolhouse where an apple tree stood. The older boys were throwing apples into the air and trying to get them go down the brick chimney. I guess a few did because Mrs. Dunnell came out back and caught the boys throwing apples. She told all of us to get inside the school and she told us we were all grounded for two recess periods. I tried to tell her that I was just watching, but to her it did not matter; I was there, so I was guilty. I complained to my mother, but to no avail.

When I got older I graduated from playing little kids games to playing horseshoes. My friend David and I were playing horseshoe one afternoon when the district superintendent Mr. Wright arrived for his monthly visit. I had thrown my horseshoes and was going to retrieve them when I heard David shout as he threw a horseshoe, "Watch me get a ringer, Mr. Wright." He did right on top of my head.

Mrs. Dunnell rushed home and got a towel to wrap my bleeding head. Mr. Wright took me home. My mother took me to a doctor in Sanford, a town ten miles away, to have my head wound stitched. I did not remember how painful the accident was, but I do remember my mother buying me a chocolate ice cream cone at Dairy Queen in town, and for me being such a "brave boy" allowing me to miss a couple of days of school. I can never forget that cut on my head, and I will never throw a horseshoe again. Today, I live miles away from David and I'm sure he never forgot that time so long ago when he was throwing a ringer and it hit right on top of my head.

I attended the Acton Corner school through fourth grade. Then the Acton school board came up with a plan to still have three one-room schools with a certain grade level.

In 1954 when I was in fifth grade I went to the Lincoln school for my last three years. We had a school bus in 1954 and the driver was Burt Clemons who was always happy. When he stopped at my home each morning he always had a smile on his face. I will never forget how kind Mr. Clemons was.

On June 1, 1957 my last elementary school year ended. That was the same year the town of Acton voted to construct a school building consisting of four rooms. On the first of May 1957 construction began and the opening was September 5th that fall. The occasion was a celebration by many teachers and students throughout York County. Thus the era of one-room school ended.

On September 4, 1957 I started my freshman year of high school in Sanford. It was a building of three levels and had more than three hundred students. It was quite a change from my little one-room school, but I adjusted. I enjoyed the hot lunch every day.

At times I think about the one-room school days and all the fun I had with all my friends. I wonder if those who are still around ever think of me.

Chapter 24
Mace Hollow, Madison Township, Armstrong Co., PA

The school was located in Kittanning, Armstrong County, Madison Township. I was at the foot doc in town when I met Robert Cortland Shuster and I asked him if he attended a one-room school as a child. I asked for his address and this is his story:

I was born at the New Kensington Hospital January 15, 1925. My parents were Robert C. Shuster and Ana Marie Rimer Shuster. I have one sister Shirley Jean who was also born at the New Kinsington hospital.

In fall of 1929 I was four and a half years old and cried to my mother to go to school. The teacher was Elvis Croyle. The school was located up an old wagon road and was full of ruts and was very muddy in winter months. Mr. Croyle told my mother to let me come to school and that year I learned my ABCs.

We lived in the country and in those days there was very little activity in our area. It was during the Great Depression and my father worked on the railroad on the Short Line between Pittsburgh and Erie. My mother had a garden and most all of our food came from that garden. Every spring Dad would purchase a small pig from a local farmer and it was my job to care for that pig during summer months. In fall the pig would be butchered for our meat during the winter months.

Mace Hollow was back in the country close to the railroad station, which was close to our home. Dad was the track foreman on the PA line and was up and ready to catch the first train out of the station at

5:00 AM along with our neighbor John who worked on the tracks. I got up early as I liked to hear the train's loud whistle as it came around the bend just before it pulled into the station. The conductor always got off the train and waved toward our home, hoping I was looking down the tracks. Mother took us to New Kensington many times to Clover Farm Store and would let us get a stick of spearmint candy out of the candy case. Mrs. Peterson would always give us two sticks.

Shirley and I walked up the hollow each morning with our little lunch pail in our hand along with Roy and Edith Wols. Edith was afraid to walk in the dark and sometimes it would still be dark in the morning. Edith talked a lot and she would ask me if I had a doughnut in my pail. She would trade anything she had in her pail for a doughnut. Mother baked the best doughnuts and raisin cookies for our pail. Mother was up early and prepared breakfast and lunch for us all. She always had a snack ready for us when we returned home from school. Dad arrived home on the 6:00 PM train.

Mace hollow had very few students and we all learned from one another. We used a slate board to do our writing. Paper was very scarce, and only the older students were allowed to write with a quill pen dipped in ink. Allie Rimer made the ink from poke berries. We did very little writing with ink during the winter months as the ink would freeze up in the ink wells. I remember when it was very cold, Mr. Murphy would let us sit around that old pot-bellied stove.

Allie Rimer was the janitor; he started the fire in the pot-bellied stove and swept the floor each morning. Beside Mr. Croyle the teachers were Josephine Fair, George Murphy, and Mrs. Brown. I loved school, and learning the requirements was what advanced me in fifth grade. I had to recite all of my multiplication tablets to be promoted. One morning I had to stand and recite my multiplication tablets and have never forgot them. Mr. Murphy told me I was a very good student and that he hoped I would do well in life—a complement I never forgot. The time Mr. Murphy spent with me has helped me to become a better person.

The town of Kittanning was growing at that time. There was a Clover Farm Store where my mother did all her shopping. She made most of our cloths out of printed feed sacks that the feed for our pig came in. There was a local farmer who delivered our milk every other day. The emptied jugs had to be returned to Bill each time he made delivery or he would ask for them. There was also a post office in town where I received a letter from the draft board that I would be drafted into World War II.

In 1943 I graduated from Kittanning High School. Along with Roy there were three other students. Dad and Mother came to the graduation ceremony, which was held at the high school. We all took the 6:00 PM train back home. Mother baked me a graduation cake, which was my favorite—chocolate with vanilla coconut icing. I invited Roy and his sister Edith to our home on Friday evening for cake and ice cream. I told Roy that I had a summer job working on the Short Line Railroad.

After graduation I started to work on Short Line from Pittsburgh to Oil City. Back then we hauled oil and coal. I did a lot of shoveling coal that summer. On September 8th I received word in the mail that I would be drafted to a government position in WWII and I was stationed for a while in the states.

I had just arrived in Japan when Pearl Harbor was bombed. I turned seventeen on January 15th and my rank was PFC. Each soldier received $21/month.

When I returned home after the war I got a job with the Army Core of Engineers as a river boat pilot on the Allegheny, Monongahela, and Ohio River. I worked as a river boat pilot for forty-two years, retiring in 1986. My wife's brother William worked with me and he drowned when he fell off one of the dams at Point Marion in 1948. He fell when he lost his balance while climbing on top of one of the dams. Emma had a hard time getting over William's death as they were very close. She didn't want William to work on the dams as she was afraid he would get hurt. Losing William was a loss in our family that was very hard to endure.

I lost my wife Emma Louise in 2001 and I presently make my home in Washington, PA. I live with a loving family who take very good care of me. I will be ninety-four on January 15th and I'm able to take care of myself and count my blessings each day.

Chapter 25
Glendale School, Dallas Pike, Ohio Co., WV

The school was located on Dallas Pike mid-way between Roneys Point and Middle Wheeling Creek. This was one of the six one-room schools located in Ohio County. The school was built in 1879 and the school colors were green and white. The school motto was "Find Your Place in God's Plan and Fill It."

I'm going to write about Margaret Elizabeth Johnson and the year was 1917. Margaret was born November 19, 1908 and was nine that fall. Her parents were George and Mary Little Johnson; her three brothers were Merle, Clarence, and Kenneth; and her three sisters were Hazel, Regenia, and Florence. Kenneth died at fifteen months of pneumonia.

Margaret's brother Merle was who she looked up to. Merle and I were very close during our years at the one-room school. Merle would sometimes carry my lunch pail when we waited for the bus each morning. Bill Guy owned a bus type wagon hitched to a team of mules and that bus hauled us kids to the Glendale school.

In winter months we had to walk most of the time. That was the year my sister Regenia started to school. There was not a lot of snow but it was very cold. My dad George took us to school in a paneled truck and often Dad carried Regenia on his back.

The teacher that year was Cordelia Orr, who lived very close to the school. Her dad brought her to school as he was the janitor. He tended the pot bellied stove which was fired by coal. Bill also swept the floor and brought in a bucket of water from the spring.

I loved the poem book that my mother gave me and carried it to school for the longest time. My mother Mary was a school teacher before she and my dad were married. Mother was from Beham, PA and taught school at the Beham Knob school. Mother taught me to recite poetry and I taught that talent to my daughter Helen who is a writer of poetry and has several poetry books in her collection.

Before each one of us kids started to school, Mother taught us our ABCs and to read out of the McGuffey primer. With all the work she had to do on the Johnson dairy farm she always found time for our education and prepared us girls for a career in teaching. Each day educating her children was always on Mother's mind.

When I was in fourth grade I got a chance to work with the first grade reading class. I remember a little boy in Regenia's class saying to me, "Margaret, you are not the teacher." His name was Billy Orr.

I had several teachers during my grade school education. I remember George G. Billick, Mary Orr, and Frank Rhodes who was my sixth grade teacher.

In sixth grade we had a box social to raise money for oil lamps that Mr. Rhodes hung along the wall. The social was at Thanksgiving time and he went to Wheeling with the money and bought eight lamps with brass brackets and hung them along the wall.

My school friends were Ruth Mitchell and Naomi Guy. Another close friend was Arma Henderson Zajak who became a teacher in the McGuffey school system. We talked about what we wanted to do when we grew up. I was thinking about becoming a teacher and Naomi didn't want to go college; she was planning on getting married.

In 1924 I was sixteen and began my studies at Tridelphia High School; the school was located on US 40 near Wheeling, WV. When I was a junior I received my class ring and it cost six dollars. That summer mother took me to visit West Liberty College; we checked all the classes and teaching was first on the list.

That fall I went with Merle to a square dance that was held at the Middle Creek school. I didn't know how to dance and I was hoping some young man would ask me to dance. I met Naomi at the dance and she was with her boyfriend.

The music was provided by Joe Walker who played the banjo, and there was an old fellow who could really play the violin or fiddle. Joe's wife played the piano. Naomi and her boyfriend were having such a good time dancing when a woman brought out a cake for the cake walk. Grab your partner and get ready to win this beautiful cake Joe yelled!

At that time I was wondering if any of the young men were going to ask me to dance when this guy with beautiful black hair asked me if would walk with him in the cake walk. It almost took my breath away as he took my hand and we began our walk. Joe yelled that there was a chalk mark on the floor and the couple standing closest to the mark will win the cake. We didn't win the cake but this young man asked me to dance. He said he didn't know how to dance and I said that makes two of us.

Turns out that he knew who I was as he had been talking to Merle. He said his name was Melvin and that he thought I was kind of cute. As we danced around the room he began to squeeze my hand and was getting way too pushy for me.

I didn't think anymore about Melvin until he pulled into the dairy barn one afternoon and wanted to see Merle, but the real visit was to see me. Merle came into the house and told me that Melvin would like to talk to me. I remember mother saying, "Is that the guy you met at square dance?" Mother's plans were for me to become a teacher.

We talked about our family and he told me he lived on a farm in Pennsylvania. He had a nice looking 1927 Chevrolet car that his dad

Harry bought him. Our first date was to visit his parents and meet his two sisters Rena and Nellie. Rena was married and had a little boy named Owen. His parents Harry and Margaret were getting ready to sit down to dinner and they invited us to join them. They owned a large dairy farm in West Finley Township not far from the town of Beham. Just before we left, Nellie and Fred stopped by with their daughter Margaret Mae. On the way back home we drove past the one-room school where my grandmother taught school.

On May 23, 1929 I graduated from Tridelphia High school and Melvin came to the graduation. On the way home Regenia rode with us and when we drove up to our driveway Regenia jumped out of the car. I was ready to invite Melvin in when he said, "Margaret, I have something to ask you—will you marry me?"

Margaret Elizabeth Johnson
Graduation, 1929

It took me by surprise, as I was planning on going to college in the fall. I couldn't wait to say yes. I knew my mother wouldn't be happy so I kept my secret until one day Mother and I were talking about my plans for college.

How was I going to tell Mother that my plans had changed and that I was not going college; I was going to marry Melvin. In just a few minutes Regenia came into the room and now I had the courage to tell Mother my plans. I didn't know how I was going to tell Mother the truth; I knew it would break her heart, so I just blurted it out. I said, "Mother my plans have changed. I'm going to marry Melvin this Christmas."

I married Harry Melvin Winters on December 24, 1929 Blacksville, WV, and have never regretted my decision to be a farmer's wife. Melvin made me a wonderful home in the beautiful country of Pennsylvania. We became the parents of two daughters—Hilda Ailes and Helen, and her husband was Robert E. Wilson. We were blessed with six grandchildren—Lourae, Dennis, Mark, Bruce, Gary, and James and one great-grandchild Christopher. We were married over fifty-two years. Melvin was seventy-seven when he died in 1982.

Chapter 26
The Depression Lesson Told by Marilyn Owens

The depression years were very difficult for most everyone. I was born in 1922 and was eight years old in 1930. I was in third grade along with my twin brother Dick. My sister Mary was several years older.

We lived on a five-acre farm in Oregon. Dad was a barber and had his own shop in town. In summer months Dad would come home after a long day at the shop and help Mama work in our vegetable garden sometimes till dark.

I didn't really know that we were poor because the farm and fruit trees yielded an abundance of food for Mama to can. Our garden yielded the best sweet corn, great big yellow tomatoes, and sweet potatoes. Dad pulled up the cabbage and buried it under straw with a old quilt covering. The celery was planted with a board siding and was covered over during the winter months.

Mama's canning skills were many. She always canned chicken and I helped her many times dressing the chickens and preparing the meat for canning. Mama had a large churn and making butter every two weeks, that was one of my jobs. The heavy cream had to be just the right consistency for churning. One of my favorite meals was served Sunday after church. We sometimes had fried chicken and Mama's peach cake.

Every morning and evening Dick's job was feeding the chickens, gathering the eggs, and milking our mow cow as Dick called her. He made pets of the chickens and gave them all a name. He didn't like any of the chickens to be butchered.

Little things that happened told me we were struggling for money. Many times dad cut out cardboard soles for our worn-out shoes. We got a new pair of shoes once a year. Mother spent her evenings in fall looking in the Sears Roebuck catalog checking prices for our shoes. We always got four pairs of socks.

One time I told dad I needed a writing tablet that would cost ten cents. He asked to see my tablet and showed me that I hadn't written on the back side of each page. I waited a long time before I got another writing tablet.

Dad could not afford to buy lunch pails for our school lunches. Mama wrapped our sandwiches in waxed paper that wonder bread was wrapped in and used newspaper and string to secure our lunch package. We took milk in a clean mustard jar.

Every summer Dick and I would go to Browns berry farm to pick blackberries. For every crate of berries we picked our tickets would be punched by one of the employees at the farm. At the end of the season we cashed in our punched tickets.

The money was used to buy our school clothes. I remember the Sears & Roebuck Catalog. Mama would help us pick out clothes we could afford from that catalog. We got our new shoes in the fall just before school started.

I also wore many used cloths that were handed down from Mary. Mama would get out her sewing basket and would add lace or buttons and make the outfits special for me. Many times long after we all were in bed I could hear the sewing machine.

Our chicken feed came in printed feed sacks. Mama didn't waist any time getting out the Singer treadle sewing machine and making Mary and I a new dress for school. She washed and ironed our pretty feed sack dresses every week for a whole year. I remember those dresses that had a lace collar and pearl buttons down the front.

Mama inherited some diamonds from her sister Ruth in 1939. With the money she went to Sears & Roebuck and bought her first surge refrigerator, which she used for over twenty years. Up till then our food went into a cooler down in the basement. I remember helping Mama defrost the refrigerator. This was done on the first Saturday of each month when Mama cleaned out the refrigerator.

Mama also had money left over to help Dick and I start our college career. We were seventeen when we graduated from high school in 1940 and started to college that September. I had decided I wanted to become a teacher and Dick was undecided at that time.

The Northwest Christian College in Eugene, OR was where we studied for four years. That is where I met Emery Owens who later became my husband. Emery and I became good friends and we were married in 1945 in Eugene, OR.

The depression years made me deeply aware of how hard Dad and Mama had to work to take care of the farm and us kids. We were taught never to waste anything. Every small piece of soap had to be saved. Every amount of leftover food would feed the animals or be placed in the cooler. Every piece of clothing had to be saved and used later on.

I saw one of my patched dresses cut up and sewed into a quilt. Mama was always busy. Whenever she would sit down she would mend, crochet, or make homemade items for the many gifts she was always making.

I look back to those early days and thank God for my dear parents, my brother Dick, sister Mary, and my home. It was much later that I realized I had actually lived through the Depression and because of that, I was better able to face challenges, hardships, and disappointments.

I learned to make do with what I had to care for our three children and our home and never wasted anything. Today I'm ninety-two years old, a retired elementary school teacher, and, I might add, the oldest choir member of my church. I look forward to continuing in this capacity for as long as possible.

Marilyn and Dick when they graduated from high school in 1940.

Chapter 27
Kimmins School, West Finley Township, Washington Co., PA

The Kimmins school was located four miles south of West Alexander on a gravel road. Mary Jane Main was born January 10, 1929 at the family home located on McGuffey Road. This is her story:

My parents were Elsworth and Carrie Craig Main. I had one sister, Evelyn, and two brothers, Glenn and Edward Main.

On September 12, 1935 I started to school. My sister Evelyn was three years older and was in fourth grade. To reach the school we all had to walk down McGuffey Road. In doing so we walked past the Sticklin home where my best friend Louise lived.

There were only four students in first grade—Louise Stricklin, Albert Daugherty, Margaret King, and myself. Our teacher Dorothy Montgomery had us all sit up front beside her desk. In first grade I learned my ABCs and learned to read in the McGuffey Primer. I learned to spell many four-letter words.

Miss Montgomery came to school each morning driving her 1934 Model A Ford and was always there during the winter months to start the pot-bellied stove. My brother Glenn and Albert Daugherty were assigned to carry in a bucket of coal and take out the ashes each afternoon just before school let out. We had to dress warm as the school house was never very warm in winter months. We girls wore long cotton stockings and rubber boots that buckled up around our ankles.

Their were twenty students enrolled. The Fry girls were Ruth, Gladys, and Mable. James Daugherty and Evelyn were in fourth grade. Ruth and Mable loved to sing and you could hear them coming down the road each morning. Mable was planning on becoming a hair stylist and she would comb and plat her sister Gladys's hair during recess. We kids walked to school in all kinds of weather; as we walked along we talked about trading our sandwiches. In fall when the concord grapes were ripe, we always grabbed a pod of grapes for our lunch. We had our own folded cups and the water from the nearby spring always tasted so refreshing at recess.

When I was in second grade we had a Christmas program and we all had parts and exchanged names. The teacher gave me a candy dish with a glass chicken on the lid and I still have that dish. We all sang "Jingle Bells" as Santa Claus came into the room and gave each one of us kids a candy cane and little box of mixed candy.

For Valentine's Day the teacher bought colored paper and we made our own valentines. It was a fun afternoon and I enjoyed using the little scissors and crayons. I made several red hearts and pasted them on white paper. Gladys was very good at art work and she cut and folded each valentine and printed our names on several cards. Miss Montgomery brought in a big box and we all helped her with the decorations. Mable, who was in eighth grade, handed out our pretty red valentines.

In 1938 was my last year at Kimmins; the school was closed and we were bussed to West Alexander grade school. I always had good grades and spelling was one of them. Every Friday we had a written spelling test. Thinking I had all my words spelled correctly, the teacher came to my desk and said, "Mary Jane, you need to look over your words and tell me which one of the words is not spelled correctly." I had blackboard spelled wrong. I never made that mistake again.

In 1946 I graduated from West Alexander High School. During all my years at the high school I became very good friends with Jean

White. Each afternoon we always had a lot to talk about in our study hall class. Jean talked about a boy she was dating and I always had Bob on my mind.

In September of my senior year Louise and I were together at the West Alexander Fair. We had strip tickets and we were riding on the merry-go-round and ferris wheel and we were always running into these three boys. They began to follow us around and Louise started to talk with them. She was boy crazy and was very anxious to find a boyfriend. Louise talked the boys into getting their pictures taken with us. The boys agreed but Bob wanted his picture taken with me and not with Louise.

In those days there was a picture taking booth set up on the fair ground. We stopped at the booth and Bob asked me if I would like to get my picture taken. He didn't ask Louise, and she got really mad. There were three pictures and she took the best one. Bob asked for my address and the very next week I got a letter from him.

After several letters he came for a visit. I was not allowed to date till I graduated from high school. When we did go to Claysville to the movie theater, Evelyn had to go with us. In 1947 we were married in the West Alexander Presbyterian Church. I had as my maid of honor my dear friend Jean White. Jean later married Duane Wilson who was from Dallas, WV.

We moved to Bob's seventy-five-acre farm on Stone Church Road near Elm Grove, WV. I was a stay-at-home mother to our daughters Evelyn, born in 1951, and Barbara, 1953. I drove our Farmall H tractor helping bring in alfalfa and clover hay for our thirty head of dairy cattle. Barbara and Evelyn helped on the farm and tended our large vegetable garden. I operated the Deval milking machine and the cooler with large paddles inside that cooled the milk. All of our equipment was run by electric power. Mr. Ball hauled our milk to United Dairy in Wheeling, WV for processing.

I did most of the farm work while Bob worked at Wheeling Electric; he was on call and left early in the morning. I lost Bob in 2012 when he was eighty-nine years old. With my quilting frame I have made over forty quilts during the cold winter months.

Today I still live on the farm and care for my great-granddaughter Abigil—we call her Abbey—while her mother works at Wheeling hospital. I have three grandchildren. God has been good to me. I count my blessings every day.

I might add that my mother Carrie told me to never marry a farmer. That was one time I didn't listen to my mother. I married Bob Davis in 1947 and he was farmer and we moved to West Virginia to his beautiful dairy farm on a hill.

Chapter 28
Davidson School, West Finley Township, Claysville, PA

The Davidson school was located between Claysville and Burnesville on a gravel road. The school got its name from the Davidson family who lived on the large farm. I will be writing about Dr. Harry Sutherland Hutchinson who was born at home on June 30, 1892. His parents were James Alexander and Ada Sutherland Hutchinson.

On September 20, 1900, Harry S. Hutchinson was in second grade, and his brother Delbert was in first grade. The teacher was Jessie Edgar. The class members were Henry Ferrell and Goldie Edger. Jessie was the older sister of Goldie.

Sixth grade members were William Hutchison, Charles Roney, and Frank Laimer. Charles Roney owned a lumber yard in Claysville. Eighth grade students were Ray Bell and Chester Sutherland. Ray Bell had his own dentist office in Claysville.

In 1900 it was very cold at Christmastime. Hazel and Etta Bell loved to sing and during the Christmas program they sang "Rudolph Red-Nosed Reindeer." Miss Edgar gave each one of us a large candy cane. School let out early for Christmas and was closed for several weeks. During recess most all the school work was done at home.

Mother Ata would visit the school often to check on us kids. Delbert was in first grade. She made peanut butter cookies several times to pass out at lunchtime. Dad had a horse that he hitched to a buggy and that was what mother drove to school and to the Clover Farm Store in Claysville to do her grocery shopping. She would always bring us kids graham crackers as we were not allowed much candy. Mother always told us candy was not good for our teeth. She took us kids to school many times in a sled as Delbert was too little to walk in the snow and she was afraid he would get sick with a cold. We wore one-piece union under wear in winter months with rubber boots buckled around our ankles. In winter, when we couldn't get out to church, she read from the Bible and taught us kids the Lord's Prayer.

Spelling class was the first subject after lunch. Miss Edgar taught us that the English alphabet consists of twenty six letters. The vowels are a, e, i, o, u, w, y. Letters are divided into vowels and consonants. The consonants are the letters that cannot be perfectly sounded without the aid of a vowel. She took time and explained all aspects of our spelling class. I didn't forget Miss Edgar's spelling instructions.

In the spring of 1910 I graduated from Claysville High School and my plan was to become a doctor of medicine. I graduated from Muskingum College in New Concord, OH. In 1920 I graduated from Western Reserve Medical School in Cleveland, OH. I did my post graduate work at Western Reserve and the medical center in Vienna, Austria.

Doc Hutchison interned at Allegheny General Hospital, Pittsburgh, PA, studied tropical decease at University of London, England, and received an honorary doctor of science degree from Muskingum College in New Concord, OH.

A member and elder of the First Presbyterian Church in Claysville, he served as a missionary in Egypt from 1921 to 1954. For the last twenty years of his medical practice, he had a office in West Alexander, PA.

Doc Hutchison was a member of the West Finley Grange and a member of the American College of Surgeons. He received a fifty-year certificate from Pennsylvania State Medical Society and was a member of the American Medical Association.

On June 23, 1921, at Presbyterian Church in Claysville, he married the love of his life Susannah McKeown. In June 1971 they celebrated their fiftieth wedding anniversary.

They were the parents of three children—James M., Ada Margaret, and Rosella who married Kenneth Nolan. Doc Hutchison died December 18, 1974.

Chapter 29
Knob School, District 68, West Finley Township, West Alexander, PA

The Knob school was located on Beham Ridge Road near the little village of Beham on John Hunter Farm. I will be writing about John Clyde Francis born June 4, 1925. His parents were John and Alta Wilson Francis and his siblings were Clara Pearl and Joyce.

Gladys E. Archer was the teacher, and the school board officers were J. L. Little, Emmett Carson, Ross Sprowls, W. D. Hutchison, and P. E. Kimmell.

Clyde was named after his mother Alta's brother Clyde who died as a small child. In the fall of 1938 Clyde was in sixth grade, Clare Pearl in fifth, and Joyce in third.

His friend was Glenn Ewing whose siblings were Lois in eighth grade and Joan in third. There were three King children—Ruby Marie in second grade and Alva and Raymond in fourth grade.

Their were nineteen students enrolled in the fall of 1937. Other students were Robert Barnes, Harold Carrell, Keith Ritchea, Opal and Irma Grinnage, Robert and Helen Archer.

Clyde and Glenn helped put up the first pole for our American flag on March 6th and all the students gathered around the pole and sang "God Bless America" with Lois Ewing conducting the singing. The Lord's Prayer was given by Clare Pearl.

Clare Pearl helped the teacher Miss Archer with the Christmas party. Mrs. Ewing came in her buggy and brought raisin cookies. Opal and Irma Grinnage sang "Jingle Bells" as Santa Claus arrived through the door and gave each one of us kids a box of crayons and a large candy stick. Miss Archer bought the crayons at Stouts store. School was dismissed for a two-week Christmas vacation. During the holidays there was a big snow and everyone was snowed in for several days. o snow With no plow to open the roads, several men grabbed shovels and went to work opening the roads.

On January 4, 1938, J. L. Little, the school president, opened the school when the roads were passable. Melvin Winters, who lived close by, hitched his team of horses to his sled and picked up the children along the school route and took them all to school. Ruby Marie King remembers the ride in the sled quite well. She sat in front of the sled with her brothers Raymond and Alva. I still remember the horses' names Bet and Brownie. Melvin had those horses trained very well to his command.

Clyde, Glenn, and Elza Clovis helped with the Halloween party. Miss Archer told us she wanted everyone to dress for the party. The Halloween costumes were sold at Clovis Store in Beham and Kimmins grocery store in Dallas, WV.

The Halloween party was held the afternoon of October 31th. Not everyone came dressed and the guessing began with the prettiest girl, funniest, and most original. Ruby Marie remembers Harold Carrell who was the funniest dressed as a clown. We bobbed for apples and Keith Ritchea bobbed one of the big red apples.

The fall of 1937 the Cooneytown school that was located on Earl Dague Farm closed and the children were sent to the Knob school. The Knob school closed the next year.

In the spring of 1938 all the one-room schools in the area were closed and students were bussed to the West Alexander school. Two students who graduated from eighth grade that year were Lois Ewing and Elzy Clovis.

A closing celebration was held the last day of school on April 22, 1938. Three members of the school board were present to hand out awards. Lois Ewing got high honors for her outstanding work helping the younger students with their multiplication tablets. As Emmett Carson handed Lois her diploma, Miss Archer pinned a beautiful pin on her dress. Robert and Helen Archer were awarded perfect attendance. Ruby Marie King, who had straight A's on her report card, was promoted to third grade. All the children were looking forward to riding the school bus that fall, and Louie King was the bus driver. That excited Ruby Marie as Louie was her father.

Clyde and Glenn finished their last two years of grade school at West Alexander. Their teacher was Mary Hupp. In 1940 Clyde graduated from eighth grade.

On April 12, 1944 Clyde enlisted in World War II. A class 3 gunner mate, he took his basic training at Norfolk, VA. He was stationed in Italy. While on the ship Clyde had to have an appendix operation and recovered in the medical unit on the ship.

Clyde's sweetheart Maxine White accompanied him to the train station in Washington, PA. Clyde was stationed in Italy for two years. Maxine graduated from West Alexander High School in the spring of 1944.

On March 1, 1949, Clyde and Maxine were married at the United Methodist Church parsonage in West Alexander. Maxine's maid of honor was her sister Jean White and the best man was Clyde's friend Robert Galentine.

Following their wedding, they took a trip to New York City on the train. They traveled to Pittsburgh to catch the 6:00 PM train on March 3rd that was headed to New York. They traveled all night reaching the city very early the next morning. They stayed at one of the hotels and enjoyed looking around the city of New York for several days.

Clyde worked for the Columbia Gas Co. The company was later named The Mountaineer Gas Co. Clyde was a meter inspector and retired in 1990 after working for the gas company forty-four years.

Clyde and Maxine are the parents of seven children—five daughters Dorothy, Sandy, Carolyn, Mary Ann, and Betty and two sons John and Mark. They have nine grandchildren and seven great-grandchildren. Clyde died June 8, 2013 at the age of eighty-seven.

John Clyde Francis, US Navy 1946, stationed in Italy.

Chapter 30
Sand Hill School, Upper Sand Hill District, Marshall Co., WV

The Sand Hill school was located four miles from Dallas, WV, on a gravel road near Sand Hill, WV. The school was one of twelve schools in the Upper Sand Hill district. Here is the story of Ruth Moss:

I was born December 31, 1926 in our farmhouse on the hill. My parents were Authur and Lila Jane Blake Moss. My siblings were my twin brother Byron (Barney) Moss and older sister Wilda Jane Moss, who married Raymond Francis of Dallas, WV.

In fall of 1931 Byron and I started to school when we were just five at the Bridge Street school in Elm Grove. Marshall County paid for us to attend the school for two years. One afternoon we were waiting in front of the school for the bus with our teacher Mable Weeks who went back into the school to pick up a book from her classroom.

While she was gone, I got the bright idea to go hunting for the bus. Byron said that the teacher told us to wait for the bus that would come and pick us up. Well I was bull-headed; I grabbed Byron's hand and off we went looking for the bus. I don't remember crossing the street but we had to as we were found near the memorial statue at Wheeling Park.

Cecil Fisher who lived with our family after his mother died was walking along on the other side of the street with his friend and happened to see us. Cecil was a student at Tridelphia High School at the time. He ran across the street and paddled me good. I was crying and I said to Cecil, "Why don't you spank Byron, too?" He answered, "Because I know who was at fault here!" He sure was right! Cecil took us home as the bus had already left when we returned to school. Mable stopped by our home that evening to check on us and Byron told her, "We went looking for the school bus and got into big trouble along the way." Cecil told mother we were lost and if he hadn't found us the Wheeling police would have picked us up and brought us home. I didn't get a spanking but I got a good talking to that evening.

In fall of 1933 we were enrolled in the Upper Sand Hill school and were in third grade. S. R. Lydick was our teacher and we had him for three years. Wilda Daugherty, who was three years older, recalls Mr. Lydick as an excellent teacher. Mr. Lydick knew the schools in the city prepared their students with projects before entering high school. On his own time he had eighth grade students doing projects—the girls made cushion covers and the boys a birdhouse.

Byron and I walked to school over a mile and a half in all kinds of weather. At recess the boys played a game of jacks that Foster Riggle carried in his pocket. We girls spent a lot of time talking to one another and jumping rope. In wintertime when the snow was on the ground, we all went outside and threw snowballs at each other.

One time it snowed over night and Mother was sure there would be no school. I was determined to go to school and out the door I went; in doing so I slipped on the ice and fell on my bottom, sliding into the pig pen that was below the house. I got up and walked to the bus stop and our neighbor told me the school bus had been canceled for the day. Back home mother was waiting for me in the kitchen with a glass of chocolate milk.

In the spring of 1936 the big flood occurred in Wheeling, WV. I was ten years old that Monday afternoon and went home with Wilda to spend the night. She had a little calf in the barn she wanted me to see. I was interested in animals and had recently joined the 4H Club at Sand Hill. I was planning on taking my two-year-old jersey cow I named Rose for my 4H project. That September dad trucked Rose to the Moundsville fair and on September 19th I entered Rose in the open dairy class and won Grand Champion. I kept that blue ribbon for the longest time.

Wilda's mother Lily had dinner ready when we walked into their home. Dale and Norval were seated at the table. They always had dinner before going to the barn to do their evening chores of milking the cows. The cows were in another pasture and they had to cross the rising waters of the creek to get to the barn.

Dale and Norval went down to the creek and drove the cows back across the flooded creek. While driving the cows into the creek and across to the other side, Dale's knee high rubber boots got stuck in the mud. Back at the barn I helped Wilda feed the baby calves, who were all bottle fed, while Dale and Norval milked their fifteen cows.

After the milking was done we walked up the hill above their home and looked down at Wheeling Island at the flooded Ohio River. As I stood there with Wilda's family I saw a sight that one would have to see to believe. Wheeling Island was completely flooded and we saw at least six homes go floating down the River.

Spelling was one subject Miss Jones was always very interested in. One Friday in April there was a spelling contest scheduled at the Dallas school. Mary Jean Riggs and I were the top spellers at the Upper Sand Hill school. Our school was let out for the day and Dad and Mom drove us to Dallas in their 1929 Dodge. Miss Jones was in charge of the contest. We all were able to spell the given words till it was my turn. The word was "engine." I was not sure whether to use i or e and my friend at the time George Milliken walked up front and was scratching his eye. I put e in the word and got it right. Mary Jean won the spelling contest and she received an honorary award from the Marshall County school board for her outstanding spelling skills.

I remember Mother putting a can of pork & beans in my lunch pail. It was winter and having a hot lunch was on my mind. On top of the pot-bellied stove is where I put the can of beans to heat them up. I didn't know at that time to punch a hole in the lid for ventilation. As we were getting ready for lunch the top of the can exploded sending beans all over the room. No beans for lunch that day! Miss Jones was really nice about the bean spill and helped all of us clean up the mess.

I graduated from Sherrard High School in 1944 and worked that summer at AP Supermarket in Elm Grove as a cashier. I stayed with Aunt Mary who lived in Elm Grove. I also worked for the Wheeling Electric Co. as a cashier for two years.

George Milliken returned home from World War II in 1946 and we began dating that spring. George was in the 723 Railroad Battalion and was stationed in Paris. He worked on a train shoveling coal and keeping the engines working. His tour of duty was for three years. He worked on the first train that crossed the Rhine River in 1943.

George and I were married September 7, 1946, at the Sand Hill Methodist Church by Rev. O. E. Elkins. I chose George's sister Betty Murdoch as my maid of honor and the best man was my brother Byron.

Our home was the farm where George grew up on Number Two Ridge Road, Dallas, WV. We were farmers and milked twenty-seven head of Jersey cows morning and evening. Before we got De Lavil milkers the cows were milked by hand. I milked all of the twenty-seven cows one evening and it took me over three hours to finish the job.

George had a heart attack in 1954 and we were able to get Lonnie Chedester to work for us. This was a time in our life that brings tears to my eyes. The man who wired our barn for electricity didn't install a ground wire correctly and during an electric storm lightning came in on the lines and killed eight of our dairy cows. Diana was so upset about the loss of the cows that she broke out in hives. I took her to doc who gave her a shot of penicillin that she was allergic to, too. Diana was in the hospital for several days.

Diana was born on July 2, 1947 and she married Bruce Armstrong their two children are Becky and Ronda. We raised four foster children Betty, Tonya, and Jimmy Sells, and Patty Roberts. Who lived with me until she died in 2008. George died October 19, 2003. I still live on our farm with my dog Molly and I wouldn't want to live anywhere else. I attend church each Sunday with several of the children.

Ruth, George, and their family. Left: Diana, Betty, Tonya, Patty and Jimmy.

Chapter 31
William Holmes McGuffey

Born September 23, 1800 and having died in Virginia 1873, William Holmes McGuffey is known as a teacher and his name will be forever associated with the series of books known as the McGuffey Reader.

His father Alexander McGuffey emigrated on August 10, 1774 from Gallaway in Wigtonshire, Scotland, a district that produced leaders in all walks of life.

Alexander McGuffey married Anna Holmes at the close of the war with the Indians in 1794. The young couple went to live with her father Henry Holmes. In 1785 William McGuffey moved to Washington County, PA and purchased a four-hundred-acre farm two-and-a-half miles from West Alexander. There he built his home, which he called "Rural Grove."

On September 23, 1800 William Holmes McGuffey was born in the Rural Grove log home in West Finley Township that fringed on an Indian trail from the Monongahela River to the Ohio River. Later it became a wagon route for the early frontiers who traveled by stage coach through this area of Washington County. He was named William after his paternal grandfather. His mother chose his middle name after her father Henry Holmes.

From 1820 to 1824 McGuffey attended Washington College now Washington & Jefferson College and taught at private school and worked on his father's farm. In 1825 and 1826 he taught in Paris, KY. On March 29, 1827 he was appointed professor of ancient language at Miami, FL. In 1829 he was ordained a minister of the Presbyterian church in the area of Virginia.

Between 1826 and 1836 McGuffey first got the idea for his readers. In the garden at the rear of his campus home he tried out his first and second readers on some of the young students as they sat on a log in the beautiful sylvan surroundings. In this way he produced those masterpieces millions have been inspired to know.

McGuffey called his works the "Electric Readers." He taught the scholars the rule of three—reading, writing, and arithmetic. He took the little ones on his knee and studied the little children's interaction. He made the first and second grade reading books small so little hands could hold them.

The sight of McGuffey's birthplace was once part of Donegal Township from which West Finley Township was taken and then divided. Dr. McGuffey was a moral philosophy teacher and lived with his wife Harriet Spining McGuffey at the University of Virginia campus for twenty-eight years from 1859 until his death in 1873.

The complete set of Electric Readers that Dr. McGuffey had published were around forty editions of some of those books. The publication dates are as followed: New High School Reader 1857, Sixth Reader 1879, Fifth Reader 1853, Forth Reader 1853, Third Reader 1843, Second Reader 1844, and First Reader 1853. He also published a spelling book that contained the alphabet with the script method, a primer, and a juvenile elocution public speaking book.

Plans in Washington County were underway in 1934 for a memorial for Dr. McGuffey. Henry Ford, who had built millions of autos, was planning on building a memorial for Dr. McGuffey whose textbooks have sold hundreds of volumes.

The log home built by Henry Holmes, grandfather of Dr. McGuffey, around 1780 is the home in which Alexander McGuffey and Henry's daughter Anna Holmes were married on December 24, 1797. This is the log home that was purchased by Mr. Ford from Etta Blayney, second cousin of Dr. McGuffey, who moved it to Dearborn, MI, in 1934. Mr. Ford then erected the present monument on the sight where the old log house stood. This monument was built in Dearborn, MI, from the stone he purchased along the Atlantic coast. The monument was brought to the sight by three craftsmen on a trailer truck accompanied by Mr. Ford and erected at the sight where William Holmes McGuffey was born in 1880.

On September 23, 1934, the largest crowd ever assembled in West Finley Township at the home of Ford, Blayney, and Holmes for the dedication of the rough stone marker for Dr. William Holmes McGuffey. It was a huge crowd of several hundred people. There were motor vehicles parked on the farm and in the field of Ralph McCleery, A. J. Roney, and the late William Patterson. Cars were parked on both sides of the road for over a mile on the Waynesburg Road known today as McGuffey Road.

Around ten o'clock Mr. and Mrs. Henry Ford arrived in their 1934 Ford along with two workers from the Edison Institute at the Greenfield Village in Michigan where Dr. McGuffey's old log home is on display. There was a lot of loud clapping as Mr. and Mrs. Ford got out of their car, and Mrs. Blayney said, "Mr. and Mrs. Ford are here today to dedicate the birthplace of one of our nation's greatest educators in modern times."

The memorial is located on McGuffey Road on the left side of the road as you travel from West Alexander, PA. The inscription on the memorial reads on the left side: "This Memorial Marks The Sight Of The Log Cabin in which William Holmes McGuffey was born September Twenty Third, Eighteen Hundred. Right side: Educator Advocate of Free Public Schools Author of McGuffey Eclectic Readers and Founder of the Graded Studied System Left side: The Birthplace of William Holmes McGuffey Right side: Restored at Edison Institute, Greenfield Village, MJ.

Around 1960 the school system in Washington County where the memorial is located built a new high school and conciliated their school and gave it a name. It didn't take the school board directors long before they came up with a new name for their school being the "McGuffey School System."